Anonymous

Pinkerton reports on CB&Q union activities, St. Joseph, Missouri, March-June 1888

Anonymous

Pinkerton reports on CB&Q union activities, St. Joseph, Missouri, March-June 1888

ISBN/EAN: 9783337732745

Printed in Europe, USA, Canada, Australia, Japan

Cover: Foto ©ninafisch / pixelio.de

More available books at **www.hansebooks.com**

Chicago, March 31st, 1888.

M. A. Stone, Esq.

Gen'l. Manager C.B. & Q.R.R.

City

Dear Sir:--

Following you will please find report of operative "J. M. W."

Thursday, March 15th, 1888.

Operative left Chicago for St. Joseph via C.B. & C. at 10.30 P.M. and continued en route during the night.

Friday, March 16th, 1888.

Operative arrived at St. Joseph at 7.10 P. M. being detained at a switch in the yards about three quarters of a mile from the Union Depot by the engineer of engine No. 28 running off of an open switch and could not get back until freight engine No. 8 coupled on the hind end of the train and pulled back on the track. No damage was done to either engine or switch that operative could see but were detained about 30 or 40 minutes. Operative had a talk with the switch tender and asked him how it happened to throw the switch wrong and he said he did not throw in front of that train, but had it set for a train that had gone East on another track and forgot to set it back for the incoming C. B. Q. train and the engineer of engine 28 whistled for the switch he simply tended to it nor of his switch shanty and switched him through without looking to see if all was as he

the switch stood and he said the fool of a "scab"ran off the switch with his eyes open, which is a fact for it was plenty light enough for the Engineer to have seen that the switch was wrong had he been paying attention to his business.

Every passenger on the train except operative got off and walked to the depot, and he remained about the engine to see what was done and what was said as there was quite a crowd of men gathered about the engine, whom operative was told were striking Engineers. He got into conversation with one of these men described as follows:

45 years old, 5 ft. 8,1-2 or 9 inches high, slim build weighing about 140 pounds, light hair and eyes and light sandy mustache wore soft hat dark pants and vest and no coat. He told operative that he was an Engineer and said that he could put that engine on the track without assistance from switch engine or any-----------

Operative remarked that he had read that the A.T. & S.F. men had all struck and that it seemed a great surprise to Arthur and all hands, officials and all. He said, "Well I have heard of something which will surprise them more than that." Operative did not ask him what he referred to, as he thought it poor policy but said he hoped it would be nothing that would prove disastrous to the Engineers' cause, and he remarked that he guessed the Engineers knew what they were about.

This man as well as the rest kept slurring the "scab" Engineer by calling him "Scabby old boy" and jeered him about the condition of his engine and windows, which in Railroad parlance was s"shut over."

Some asked him why he did not have curves put in his stack, others said he must be a "hay seed" and to all of these jeering remarks the "scab" Engineer made no reply. When engine 49 and train pulled up behind this train, the Engineer with the birth mark said he would give $10. to see her go crashing into the passenger train to dump the w'ole train in the ditch. Operative said,"you would not wish to see any one hurt, would you?" he said, "No, none of the passengers, but they are all out and have walked down to the depot."

Two Rock Island switch engines that were held there as their crossing was blocked kept up a continual tooting of their whistles which were made to resemble groans as much as could be, and did so after the engine was on the track and the crossing cleared.

Operative went to the St. Charles hotel and registered and after supper went to see Mr. Merrill who told him that it was not to look up anything that had been done, that he sent for a man, but to learn if anything was going to be done. He said such dirty tricks as soaping tanks, blocking crossheads and putting Emery on the guides had been tried and as yet no damage had resulted from the attempts, save considerable annoyance; he said he knew how very secret the Brotherhood were and appreciated the fact that operative had an up hill task before him, and did not know if he could accomplish much, but he wanted him to try it as long as he thought it advisable, and that if after a few days he decided that he could do no good, he could then discontinue.

Mr. Merrill told operative not to communicate with him unless he had some information to impart, and then to do so by mail, but if he learned anything that he thought he ought to know at once, then to call at his house at night; he said he wanted to get some hitch on some of the men so he could put them in jail for a time, as he thought that would tend to put a stop to hostilities quicker than anything, and he mentioned in this connection the shooting of the engineer at Brookfield by the Deputy Sheriff and said that served as an effectual quietness more than anything else had done, but did not want it to come to pass here. He told the operative to hang around the depot

their eyes regret operative's presence. There are also a numbe of traitors, who according to Mr. Grasely's opinion whom operative and his we will endeavor to watch as far as possible. There are generally men who drop off from every incoming train and have some mysterious jotting with one or more of the local strikers in some quiet corner, ostensibly to keep the men posted about what there is going on at headquarters and what is going to be done in the future.

Dissatisfaction prevails and some trouble may be the result.

Yours respectfully,

Pinkerton Nat'l. Detective Agency

by W. A. Pinkerton

Gen'l. Supt. W. Div.

K.B.

Chicago, March 24th, 1888

M. D. Stone, Esq.

Gen'l. Manager C.B. & Q.R.R.
City

Dear Sir:--

Following you will please find report of operative
"D. H. W."

Saturday, March 17th, 1888

To-day in St. Joseph

Operative only visited the Union Depot twice to-day, and although he had some conversation with some of the employees about the strike, yet he learned nothing of any importance whatever.

Operative took the side of the Engineers to see if he could draw them out; said his sympathies were them, but yet he considered their chances very slim to win the fight unless they were given assistance from outside railroad men and operative is sured that every engine or who struck would and the Brotherhood's chances of winning at the rate of $ per th at least. Operative found no opposition to his chances, at least no... ..., but those to whom a talks to him either rided in with his views. He did not take any great in talking as he is afraid to would attract attention and might cause suspicion. He also had that talkk with the men of it is known as the spot car as he had finished about the that the switch on vay and of the engineer ith the rth rk. He driver said he his fines few on it also

Operative asked the Engineer's name. The car driver could not say, he had heard it but had forgotten it.

There are a great many Railroad men stopping around the St. Charles hotel and operative spends a great deal of his time around the house trying to get acquainted, as it were, and did get on speaking terms with two or three men he knows are Railroad, yet he did not learn either their names or the particular branch of Railway work they follow. Operative did not see these men until 8 P... and then they were just going out of the hotel. Operative asked them if there was to be a dance, thinking they might be going there, but they did not say. Operative learned further during the evening.

Sunday, March 18th, 1888

Operative was at the train at 1.30 P. M. at the arrival of the Kansas City, St. Joseph and Council Bluffs train and saw two young men who from their actions appeared to be Railroad men, as they tried to get either a look at or word to the Engineer of the train. As soon as the train pulled out two young men went away going south on 6th St. about three blocks from the depot and entered a house with no number on. Operative shadowed them so far in hopes that he might locate them in some boarding house. Although the house had no number on it still after waiting about one hour operative made inquiry of a lady who came to the door if she knew of any boarding houses near there, or if she could not or would not take a boarder. He was told no and so went away. Operative played pool with some of the strikers at the St. Charles hotel to-day but all to no purpose as he did not even learn the names of the parties with whom he was playing.

Operative went to the Post office to see if there was a letter for Mr. L. P. Merrill, but as yet no word has come.

Yours respectfully,
Pinkerton Nat'l. Detective
by W. S. W.
Nt.'l. Supt. W. Div.

Chicago, March 27th.88

H.B.Stone Esq.,
  Gen'l.Mngr.C.B.& Q.Ry.
   City.

Dear Sir.,

  Following you will please find report of operative
"E.H.W."

          Monday, March 19th.88

To day in St.Joseph,

    The operative received a letter from Gen'L manager Merril giving him the names of three Engineers viz.D. C.Pierce, C.E.Patterson, and Richard Morris, who he said had been threatening violence, that they had threatened Pat Burns Engineer and his Fireman who are the only two of the company's old men who stood by them during this trouble, and also Engineer Saege was threatened.

    The operative located these men "is" Patterson and Morris at 2135 and 2137 So.6th. St., which is a double two story brick house. Pierces address he could not get.

    The operative answered Mr.Merrill's letter and asked him to give him the address of the men whose names he had given him, as their caller has them. The operative made this request so as to be sure he was right, as any of them may have changed from the address given in the directory. He found the directerEugene Martin's name and he is given as roomer ing at 1302 So.10th. St., so the operative went down to the vicinity of this house and found there is no sign nor indications of any kind that furnished rooms are for rent or board given, it looks like a private residence, and no more than likely is, and that Martin is a friend and acquaintance of the family, and so is accommodated with a room. In the directory he also found that F.P.McDonald "Fireman" is supposed to room at 2220 So.Sixth St., and he found this house a double two story frame building with no appearances of being a furnished room house, and no signs to that effect, and as he did not know for certain whether either McDonald or Martin roomed as given in the directory, he made no effort to get into either of these houses, thinking it best to wait until he heard from Mr.Merril to see if the addresses he gets from the caller compares with those given in the directory.

The operative went into A.E.Amells saloon in the vidinity of 2135 So.6th. St., where e had a game of cards with four or five men. There was a general conversation on Railroad matters and the Sante.Fe.strike was discussed, each man giving him opinion of the result that would be, but nothing of importance came up, and no one seemed to be better informed than the other. They said five or six of the Brotherhood Engineers from the 'Q.'Ry.had gone to work on the Chicago Kansas & Nebraska Ry, but no names were mentioned.

The operative played until 11:30 p.m. then quit having lost three games. He remained in the vicinity of 2135 So.6th. St.,until 12:30 p.m. expecting he would see some man entering either that number or 2137 which which he thought w would either be Morris or Patterson. The operative saw no one however and so returned to the St.Charles Hotel.

About 3 p.m. the operative again went to xxx Arnell's saloon
but found no one in, so after taking a glass of Beer he went
out and located Mr. Sullivan's house 2212 So.6th. St., Thos.
Reynolds 1314 So.6th. St., C.L.Gressoups 1614 So.9th. St., but
saw no men about either place.

            Tuesday, March 20th.88

   To day the operative received no reply from the Genl
Manager Mr. Merrill as yet. He was down in the vicinity of
2135 and 2137 So.6th. St., to day at 12 noon, and remained in
that neighborhood until 12:45 p.m. but saw no men entering
either of those numbers. At 2 p.m. he again went down on
So.6th. St., and entered A.E.Anell's saloon where he purchased
a Cigar and had a friendly talk with the bartender on general
topics, only touching on the Sante.Fe.Ry.strike and not saying
a word about the "C.B.&.Q. trouble, except to argue against his
opinion which was; that the brotherhood would never be recogniz
ed on the Q.Ry.system again. After remaining there a short
time the operativ went to the depot where he remained about
30xx minutes, and everything being "dead"he returned to the hos
tel.

   After supper the operative played Pool with a Conduc
ton named Pinger and an Insurance Agent named Drew. The lat
ter represents the Travelers accident Indurance Co.of Hart
ford Conn. and is at work among the new Engineers on the K.C.&
St.J.and C.B.& Q.Ry.and hears considerable talk pro.et.con.
as to the "Q".Ry.the brotherhood and its chances of success.

   After playing a few games the operative picked up
the Daily News and read the article aloud which says the "Q".
Ry' Co.has 1000 crews (Engineers & Firemen)engaged and had in
structed his Eastern & Canadain Agents to send no more, and al

so that the 'Q.'Ry.was supplying the Central Iowa Ry.with Engineers and Firemen from the overflow. This started the conversation on Ry.topics,and during its progress Drew said that he knew one Engineer new (who was fireing for a brotherhood man before the strike and would not go out with the rest of them he (the fireman) not being a brotherhood man).and that this man told him that five of the brotherhood Engineers had left,and gone to Wymore to take positions there,thus showing that their belief in the success of the strike was loosing grounds. Harry (Bartender in St.Charles Hotel Bar) said he thought every one could get back . But Drew said he got it straight from the Master Mechanic and Round House Foreman of the K.C.shops that not one of the new men who were capable to handle his engine would be discharged,and that the brotherhood is "dead on" to the Q.road. Lee another bartender at St.Charles Hotel said that his brother-in-law Frank Pritchard who is Conductor on the K.C.& St.J.& C.B.Ry.said he thought that the way the boys (Brotherhood)men)had talked that they had given up all hopes of wining their fight,but most of them thought they would be given their old places back especially the Passenger Engineers. Drew said,'Well you will see that none of them get back,and but very few if any at all.'.

Wednesday,March 21st.88

This morning the operatie recevád two letters from Gen'l.Mngr.Merrill one telling him that he was called to Kansas City for a few days,and the other giving the addresses of some of the striking Engineers which prove to be the same as the operative got from the directory,so after dinner he started out to see what his chances were of getting located where he would be thrown more in contact with the Engineers.

therefore thought he would make an effort to get into 2220 where McDonald rooms. He went to 2218 and inquired for board and room. Mrs.Evans who runs this borading house said she could furnish him with board and room if he would occupy a room with 3 beds in it. This, the operativ would not lise ten to and asked her about her neighbors,if they did not have rooms to rent that he could get and take his meals with her. She said no,because she knew the rooms were all full. The operative asked her what her boarders principally were,and what business they followed? She said railroading and then went on to say that the men in the room are Machinists, and in such a one Engineers, and that in 2216 was a Carpenter and in 2220 a couple of firemen who all took their meals with her.

   She directed the operativ to two rooms on the outside one on the corner of 23rd.St.,or where 2300 would begin, and the other in the same block,on same side of the street and only three doors from where Engineers Morris and Patterson live, She said that Mrs.Stacey lives there and has a good front rom for rent,at least did have a few days ago. She also said she used to rent her rooms out before she began taking boarders, and thought it paid nearly as well for s he used to get $12 to $18 dollars per month,and she thought the operative would have to pay that much for either tof those rooms she referred him to, then asked him if he had a partner,and the operative told him not here at present,but if he got located all right he had a friend who would come on here.

   The operative went over to Mrs.Stacey's and saw the room,she had given the refusal of tit to a Machinists who was to let her know either tonight or tomorrow night,whether he would take it or not ,and said if he did not take it operative could have it. The operative thinks this location will be a good one, for he will no doubt be thrown in direct contact with F.P.McDonald (the foreman)who the operative has no doubt is one of the men Mrs.Evans referred to as rooming in 2220 So.6th. St, and taking his meals with her, and again being so close to Morris and Patterson it seems as though he must run against them through some acquaintance he is bound to make at Mrs.Stacey's and Mrs.Evans.

After leaving Mrs.Stacey's the operative stepped in John Miller's saloon and while talking to Miller about John L.Sullivan's fight with Mitchell which topic they took up from the fact of Miller having the Police Gazette in his hand when the operative entered.

After the talk about the Sullivan and Mitchell fight the operative got him started on the strike, by commenting on the Santa.Fe.& Missouri Pacific's announcing themselves ready to handle C.B.& Q.Freight. Miller (at least the operative heard him called John and sign ready John Miller's place(said he did not see how the boys could prevent them from handling C.B.& Q.freight,unless it would be to lay down their tools entirely,and then he added the C.B.& Q.would be reaping a rich harvest,for no doubt she would do a double increased business.

It is claimed that Miller has read the arguments made by Geo.Martin in Topeka before the brotherhoods committee in his disapproval of the claims made by the men,and now uses nearly the same arguments himself. The operative said the boys could torment the life out of the C.B.& Q.officials by resorting to voilence in some instances and other tricks known to the trade if they chose to." Miller said he did not believe they would stoop to any such means of winning their bat-

tle, but did think they would employ any honorable means to
harrass the 'Q.'people just as Chairman Conroe stated. He
also said he did not believe the C.B.& Q.would ever recognize
the brotherhood again,and he thought there were a number of
old Engineers that would never do any more railroading,and when
asked why;because a number of them are pretty well fixed and
own their own homes and rather than to sell out and go to some
new country,would gradually get into some other business or em
ployment.

       In the evening the operative went down to A.E.Amell's
saloon and got into a game of Pool with the bartender and re=
mained there until 8:30 p.m. and then left. There were sev=
eral people in the saloon,but the operative heard no Ry.talk
of any consequence. The operative also had another talk with
Drew (the Insurance Agent)and he said that the 5 or 6 men he
spoke of going to Wymore did not get work,that they were in=
formed there was no work for them.

                                           Thursday,March 22nd.88

       This forenoon the operative went down to A.E.Amell's
saloon on So.6th. St.,below the S.J.& G.Island Round House
and remained there about three quarters of an hour talking
with the bartender and a brakeman of the St.J.& Grand Island
Ry.named Pratt. The operative told him that he believe the
strike was virtually was over. He said,the strike is far
from being over ,the Switchmen are going to quit because they
will not work behind the new and incompetent Engineers .
The operative told him he was satisfied the Engineers did not
expect their assistance,and that he thought the Sitchman had
better work on the old addage and wait until they had been called upon for assistance.

The operative here...
ed that John Miller does not run this saloon now, but has sold
it out to some man they call George who is a great dog fancier.
They got in conversation about his dogs, then drifted to the
strike. George said, "I am sick of talking about it there has
Been no strike, the Engineers simply quit and let the company
fill their places with other men "Scabs".

In the afternoon the operative again went down to
Millers and played several games of "seven up"with George and
two other men whose names he did not learn as he left the saloon before they did and had no chance to ask the Proprietor
who they were.

At 7:30 p.m. the operative again went down on So.6th.
St., and this time saw Mr.& Mrs.Stacey and learned that the man
had disappointed them about taking their room. The operative
therefore paid them the price asked and took the key saying
he would move in sometime during the day tomorrow. As he
was going back up town he called into the saloon (no name)
2116 So.6th. St., just across the street from his room and had a
glass of beer and asked the proprietor to join him, and then
told him he was a neighbor of his and he would expect him to
use him pretty well. The operative done this simply to get
on friendly terms with him, not knowing but his saloon may be a
resort for some of the Engineers and Firemen.

Friday, March 23rd.88

To day the operative moved from his room in the St.
Charles Hotel to his room at 2119 So.6th. St., this a.m. and
went over to Mrs.Evans Boarding house (2218 So.6th. St.,) and
told them he would take his meals with them.

At the dinner table the operative met some Engineers

Firemen and Switchmen, but was not introduced to them, and he did not care to make himself too fresh, so said little. During the afternoon he spent his time between his room and Miller's saloon where he played several games of cards with the proprietor and a couple of C.K.& N.Brakemen, but learned nothing more than a rumor that before long the Switchmen and Brakemen were going out on the C.B.& Q.Ry.

At 5:30 p.m. the operative again went to Mrs.Evans boarding house where he met Miss Evans and gave her the details of the whipping of Pat Brown as he got it from the 'Evening News' and mentioned the names of Chripopher and Whaley Firemen and Roderick and Morris Engineers, and of course took the side of the Engineers and said they served him (Brown) right, and the only thing he blamed them for was for doing such a thing in broad day light, so they could be recognized and get arrested which according to the papers account would be done, in fact opeative added Roderick has already been arrested. Miss Evans said he knew Charley Roderick very well and did not think he would do such a thing, although he is big enough to whip 3 or 4 men himself without any help. She said that Pat Brown had been turned out of the brotherhood for drunkness and the company would not give him an engine to run before the strike, on that account but kept him on a switch engine and when the strike came he was given the best engine (No.4) on the road and that Charley Thomas No.4's former Engineer said he believed the company sent the 4 out first just to tantalize him as they knew that he thought a great deal of his engine . She also said that Charley Teppin Engineer followed his engine two or three trips to Kansas City on purpose to whip the engineer who is now running it, and that he attempted to whip the Conducto

Miss Evans showed the operative her album and along side of her Photo.was that of John Hopkinson a Fireman on the K.C.St.J. and C.B.Ry. The operative joked her about the position John occupied off the road (her escort or steady company) and she said no,that is not it,but John was an old freend of the family's having come from Pottsville Pa.where they lived until 2 years ago. Hopkinson came in at that moment and Miss Evans said,"Oh;John,what do you think I heard?" She then related how Brown had been whipped and added that Rederick had been arrested and that warrants were issued for Morris and others. John asked her who said so? Miss Evans said this gentleman (the operative) was just telling me,he read it in the evening news. John said,"Well it is a mistake,the papers dont always know everything". Mrs.Evans said,"No,but I'll bet you know all about it. John told her not to ask him anything about it. Mrs.Evans said,"Oh you need not fear,I know you too well to ask you anything about it. She then continued (after John had gone up stairs)"Why I was over to Mrs.Morris's this afternoon and she did not say anything about it,"

At the supper table the subject was again brought up and a sandy headed and red mustacheed Switchman (dont know what yard or for what company he works)spoke up and said,"Pitty the boys did not finish the job when they had it started John Hopkinson said,"Yes,it would not have cost us any more." The switchman told of some engine that had been disabled (39 think he said)and Hopkinson said he wished they would all get crippled. The operativ did not take an active part inthe conversation,but said enought to give those present to understand he was with them .

Miss Evans said that her Papa and Mama were going to see the Arabian Nights at Tootles Opera House, and asked the operative if he was going. The operative told her he did not care to go alone. She told him to go with them as they would be glad to have his company. The operatve thought this would be a good way we get their good graces, and so said if he would not be in the way he would like to accompany them. Mrs. Evans then said that perhaps John (Hopkinson) would go along with them. They went, but John did not go with them. He seems an odd young man looks down at the flood most of the time, when talking or else over your head, cant look a person in the eye at all Nothing new turned up to report on their trip to the Opera House and return.

                                        Yours Respectfully,
                               Pinkerton's Natl Detective Agency.
                                           by. *[signature]*
                                          Genl Supt. W. Div.
                                                   A. C.

Chicago, March 28th, 1888

H. B. Stone, Esq.
    Gen'l. Manager C.B. & Q.R.R.
        City

Dear Sir:--

    Following you will please find report of operative
"L. F. W."

           Saturday, March 24th, 1888

To-day in St. Joseph.

    Operative took his meals at Mrs. Evans' Boardig House to day and met John Hopkinson and several other firemen, still he was unable to learn anything of an important nature.

    Railroad topics were the general conversations, but only general topics were discussed. Operative did not get an opportunity to speak to Mrs. Evans or her daughter at any time during the day. Operative sent W. F. Merrill a line explaining his location, and gave it as his belief that John Hopkinson had a hand in or knew all about the shooting of Pat Brown. Operative spent some time in John Miller's Saloon, but the conversation was principally about hogs, he could not get him talking about the strike.

    Operative made two trips to the Post office, but received no mail, also went to the Gold Dust Saloon opposite the Union depot at about 7.00 P.M. and saw two railroad men there whom he recognized

    Wife of Mr. Evans. Operative said in a half complaining way I hope the strike will soon be over, one way or the other, for I am tired of doing so. He was asked in he come here to go to work, said no, he did not for if he had he could have been working the past two weeks. Operative then said he thought a man of principle would show that principle whether bound by a secret organization, or obligation or not, and one of the men said he believed that was so, and that a man without a principle could not be a good Knight of Labor or a good Brotherhood man. These men operative thinks are switchmen in the Kansas City yards and left the saloon, taking a car up town saying, well we will see you again. Operative then left the saloon and discontinued.

    Yours respectfully,

      Pinkerton Nat'l. Detective Agency

       by W. F. Pinkerton

        Gen'l. Supt. W. Div.

          K.B.

ST. PAUL, UNION BLOCK,　　KANSAS CITY, 106 & 107 WEST SIXTH ST.,
W. J. LOADER, SUPT.　　　　C. H. EPPELSHEIMER, SUPT.

Chicago, April 4th.88

H.B.Stone Esq.,

    Gen'l.Mngr.C.B.& Q.R.R.

        City.

Dear Sir.,

    Following you will please find report of operative
"E.H.W."

                    Tuesday,March 27th.88

To day in St.Joseph,

        This morning the operative went to the Post Office , but as he received no letters went back to 6th. St., to the Gold Dust saloon, and remained there for about an hour, but as he could learn nothing of importance he left.

        After supper Pillson and John Hopkinson called at the operative's room, and they left to go to the Dime Museum. Pillse spoke of the Conductor that was killed in the collision early this morning, and said that was some of the good Engineer work the accident and death of the Conductor in question came about in this way-'As the operative is informed, the freight train broke in two pieces, the Conductor was on the rear car , and in backing up the Engineer ran at the rate of 20 miles per hour,-so fast at least'that when the rear half of the train was sighted'they could not stop the engine and cars with it, and when the crash came the Conductor was thrown off and run over, and one of the box cars in falling fell upon him.

The operative told him he thought the brotherhood's 'cake was all dough' and they shortly would be obliged to admit it. Pillson argued that the assistance rendered by the Chicago Switchmen would materially change things in the brotherhood's favor and he appealed to John to know if that was not the way the Engineers looked at it, and John said yes. The operative said, "Well you have my sympathy and all that, but I cant bring myself to believe that one hundred or two hundred Switchmen's going out in Chicago is going to win this fight for you in St. Joseph, Council Bluffs, Lincoln, and Plattsmouth etc. and I think you are clinging to a forlorn hope, and the sooner you see it so, the better."

John said that the Switchmen and Brakemen in Council Bluffs had already gone out, and the operative asked him if they claimed any grievances, or if it was simply out of sympathy for the Engineers cause. John said it was done simpl to help the brotherhood, Pillson said the Switchmen here were expecting an order to quit at any time. John said probably nothing would ne done until Thomas and McDonald returned from Chicago where they had gone. (left to day) The operative told him what he had previously said had not been with an aim to offend nor discourage, but simply expressed his views, as he felt he had a right to do; but that he sincerely hoped his predictions would not come true. Pillson said the brotherhood plainly saw death to the brotherhood in losing this present struggle, and would no giv. p as long as there was a possible show for wining. This ended the conversation until they had been to the Gold dust saloon and had drinks and Cigars, and as they were about the Kansas City Tracks (north of depot) a K.C. Passenger train pulled out, and John said, "Go it, 'Scab"S--

of a B----and turning to Pillson he said,"I wonder if I will ever have the pneasure of holdng down an engine for the K.C. company again. He said,'Oh yes,I think so.' They then went to their rooms.

The operative did not call upon Mr.Merrill to inform him of the contemplated movement among the Switchmen here,for according to John's statement nothing was to be done until Thomas & McDonald returned from Chicago.

Yours Respectfully,

Pinkerton's Natl Detective Agency

by. *W. A. Pinkerton*

Genl Supt.W.Div.

A.C.

Pinkerton's National Detective Agency

OFFICES
- CHICAGO, 191 & 199 FIFTH AVE., WM. A. PINKERTON, SUPT.
- DENVER, OPERA HOUSE BLOCK, JAS. [illegible], SUPT.
- PHILADELPHIA, 45 SOUTH THIRD ST., R. J. LINDEN, SUPT.
- NEW YORK, 66 EXCHANGE PLACE, GEO. D. BANGS, SUPT.
- BOSTON, 42 & 44 COURT ST., JOHN CORNISH, SUPT.

ATTORNEYS FOR THE AGENCY:
CLARENCE A. SEWARD, NEW YORK.
LEWIS C. CASSIDY, PHILADELPHIA.
D. W. MUNN, CHICAGO.

FOUNDED BY ALLAN PINKERTON 1850
WM. A. PINKERTON, Gen'l Supt. Western Division, CHICAGO.
ROBT. A. PINKERTON, Gen'l Supt. Eastern Div. NEW YORK.
"WE NEVER SLEEP."

CONNECTED BY TELEPHONE.
ST. PAUL, UNION BLOCK, W. J. LOADER, SUPT.
KANSAS CITY, 106 & 107 WEST SIXTH ST., C. H. EPPELSHEIMER, SUPT.

CHICAGO, APRIL, 6TH. 1888.

H. B. STONE, ESQ.,
    GENL. MNGR. C. B. & Q. RY.
        CITY.

DEAR SIR,

    FOLLOWING YOU WILL PLEASE FIND REPORT OF OPERATIVE "S. H. Y".

        THURSDAY, MARCH 29TH. 88.

TODAY IN ST. JOSEPH.

    TODAY THE OPERATIVE RECEIVED TWO LETTERS FROM GENL. MNGR V. F. MERRILL, ASKING HIM IN THE FIRST IF HE WAS DOING ANY GOOD, FOR THE ROAD, AND IN THE SECOND HE STATED THAT IN HIS ESTIMATION, THE SWITCHMEN, SHANNON AND DICKEY'S., EVIDENCE BEFORE THE CORONER, WAS, FALSE. HE REQUESTED OPERATIVE TO TRY AND OBTAIN INFORMATION THAT WOULD SHOW WHERE THEY PERJURED THEMSELVES.

    THE OPERATIVE REPLIED TO THE FIRST LETTER, BY SAYING THAT HE WOULD MAKE AN EARNEST ENDEAVOR TO DO SOME GOOD. THE OPERATIVE IS TAKING HIS MEALS IN THE SAME HOUSE WITH ASST. YARD MASTER HOOTON, AND ONE OTHER SWITCHMAN, AND THOUGHT THE LOCATION WAS IN HIS FAVOR, AS HE COULD PERHAPS LEARN SOMETHING FROM THESE MEN. HOOTON SAID HE THOUGHT ALL THE $2.00 A DAY PINKERTON MEN WERE COWARDS, AND THAT IF SOME ONE WAS TO PASS THROUGH THE YARDS, AND RAP LOUD ON A BOX CAR, WITH A CLUB, THEY WOULD ALL SCATTER. THE OPERATIVE SUGGESTED THAT HE TRY IT SOME NIGHT, BUT HE SAID "NO".

    HE SAID THE NEW ENGINEERS(SCABS HE CALLED THEM) WOULD WIN THE SWITCHMENS FIGHT BY KILLING OFF ENOUGH OF THE NEW SWITCHMEN

TO SCARE THE OTHERS OUT. HE ALSO SPOKE OF THE ONE ARMED MAN THE COMPANY HAD EMPLOYED TO SWITCH, AND SAID, " THAT SHOWS WHAT THE COMPANY WILL RESORT TO. HE RIDICULED THE IDEA OF THE ONE ARMED MAN SWITCHING, AND SAID "TWO ARMS WERE NEVER IN HIS WAY. AND OFTEN TIMES HE FOUND THAT THREE WOULD BE AN IMPROVEMENT.

AT 8. 35 P. M. THE OPERATIVE PROCEEDED TO THE UNION DEPOT, AND SAW THE TWO STRIKING SWITCHMEN HOOTON AND HURLEY, ON THE DEPOT PLATFORM WITH A CROWD OF 10 OR 15 RY. MEN. HE JOINED THEM, AND LEARNED THAT THEIR CONVERSATION WAS FOR THE MOST PART ABOUT PINKERTON DEPUTY SHERRIFFS, WHO HAD ARRIVED FROM CHICAGO. IT WAS FREELY REMARKED THAT THEY WISHED HUNDREDS MORE WOULD BE SENT, FOR IT WOULD CAUSE THE RY. COMPANY TO BORROW MORE MONEY THAT IT WAS NOW DOING. IT IS GENERALLY REMARKED, AND BELEIVED THAT THE COMPANY ARE BORROWING MONEY TO CARRY ON THE STRIKE, AND THIS IS TAKEN AS A GOOD OMEN FOR THE STRIKERS ULTIMATE SUCCESS.

HOOTON SAID, HE WAS IN THE NOTION OF FIXING UP A DUMMY FOR THE PURPOSE OF PLACING IT BEFORE THE G-----. D---S---OF--A--B---ENGINE THAT KILLED CHARLEY FRANCIS, ON APRIL FOOLS DAY, AND SEE IF IF HE COULD NOT SCARE THE SCABS OUT OF THE YARD. IT WOULD HARDLY PAY EITHER HE THOUGHT, FOR HE SAID THE FOOLS WOULD NOT HAVE SENSE ENOUGH TO SEE IT.

FRIDAY, MARCH 30TH. 88.

THE OPERATIVE DID NOT SEE HOOTON OR HURLEY TODAY. BOTH TRAVEL TOGETHER, AND ATTEND THE MEETINGS OF THE BROTHERHOOD TWICE DAILY, WHICH IS OPEN TO ALL STRIKERS, WHETHER BROTHERHOOD MEN OR NOT. JOHN HOPKINSON A FIREMAN, WHO VISITED OPERATIVES ROOM DURING THE EVENING, SAID HE WAS NOT A BROTHERHOOD MAN, BUT, THAT IN ASMUCH, HE WAS ADMITTED TO THEIR MEETINS, EXCEPT THE PRIVATE ONES WHICH WERE HELD TWICE A WEEK, FOR MEMBERS ONLY.

THE FIREMAN SAID THAT ONLY TODAY THEY HAD ENCOURAGING NEWS

FROM CHICAGO, AND WERE CONFIDENT OF WINNING THE STRIKE, AS IT WAS ONLY A MATTER OF A FEW DAYS, BEFORE THE C. B. & Q. PEOPLE WOULD HAVE TO ADMIT THEY WERE BEATEN.

THE OPERATIVE RELATED TO THE FIREMAN, THE NEWS ABOUT THE BURNING OF THE PAINT SHOP, AND BOARDING HOUSE USED BY THE ENGINEERS, AND FIREMEN AT AURORA. HOW THE MEN BARELY ESCAPED WITH THEIR LIVES &C &C. HE SAID, " OH, THATS BROTHERHOOD WORK SURE ENOUGH. SERVES THEM RIGHT, THEY OUGHT TO BE BURNED.

SATURDAY. MARCH 31ST. 88.

THE OPERATIVE ATTENDED THE MEETING OF THE BROTHERHOOD IN COMPANY WITH TWO YOUNG MEN. THE MEETING HAD COMMENCED WHEN THEY ARRIVED, AND JUST BEFORE, THE EDITOR OF THE DAILY GAZETTE WAS TEARING THE AIR IN AN OPEN DENOUNCEMENT OF THE C. B. & Q. COPORATION.

HE TOOK UP THE ENGINEERS HERE AND CRIED AGAINST THE PINKERTON DETECTIVES, SAYING "WHO SENT THEM HERE", PROBABLY TO OVERCOME SOME ONE, AND WHAT OUGHT TO BE DONE WITH THEM." HE ASKED WHO IS THIS PINKERTON, AND HE ASNWERED THE QUERRY HIMSELF SAYING "HE IS THE PRINCE OF LIARS", AND THAT 'HIS DETECTIVES (WITH A SNEER) WERE A LOT OF PAID LIARS, AND THEIVES. THE OPERATIVE HAD HEARD ENOUGH OF SUCH TALK, AND WITH HIS COMPANIONS LEFT THE MEETING AND VISITED VARIOUS PLACES AROUND THE TOWN.

THE TWO MEN IN COMPANY WITH OPERATIVE JOHN HOPKINSON AND DILLSON, BEGAN TALKING ABOUT CORCORIANS SPEECH, SAYING HE HAD MISREPRESENTED THE FACTS WHEN HE SAID THERE HAD BEEN NO VIOLENCE RESORTED TO ON THE PART OF THE STRIKERS, AND ALLUDED TO PAT BROWN, BEATIBG ,MERELY HAVING HIS EARS BOXED. THEY SAID HE FAILED TO MENTION ABOUT TOPPINS HITTING THAT POOR INOFFENSIVE BOILER MAKER OVER THE EYE WITH A POOL BALL, AND HE (TOPPIN) SURROUNDED BY A DOZ- -EN OR MORE FREINDS. THEY SAID WHILE THE ARABAIN NIGHTS COMPANY WERE PLAYING THERE THAT 11 SCABS WENT TO THE OPERA HOUSE TOGETHER AND CAME BACK WITHOUT GETTING' DONE UP.,' BECAUSE THERE WAS ENOUGH

OF THEM TO TAKE CARE OF THEMSELVES. "TOPPIN" THE MAN WHO THREW THE ENGINEER OVER THE BRIDGE IN KAS. CITY SAID HE WOULD "LICK" EVERY MAN, WHO TRIED TO RUN HIS ENGINE.

ONE OF THE MEN WHOSE SYMPATHY IS WITH THE STRIKERS, SAID HE DID NOT BELEIVE IN CRIPPLING MEN FOR LIFE, AND HIS OPINION WAS THAT THE ENGINEERS WERE NOT AS GOOD AS HE FIRST THOUGHT THEY WERE HE SAID THEY WERE TOO WILLING TO ACCEPT AID FROM BRAKEMEN, & SWITCHMEN, WHILE AT FIRST, THEY SAID "THIS IS OUR FIGHT, AND THAT THEY DID NOT WANT ANY HELP FROM OUTSIDE SOURCE", WHILE NOW IT WAS "GOOD BREAKMEN, GOOD SWITCHMEN, GOOD ANYBODY, WHO WAS WILLING TO HELP THEM. PERSONS THAT DID NOT HELP THEM WERE CALLED SCABS.

BEFORE RETIRING FOR THE NIGHT THE OPERATIVE VISITED VARIOUS PLACES WHERE THE STRIKERS LOITER, BUT REPORTED NOTHING FURTHER OF INTEREST.

YOURS RESPECTFULLY.

PINKERTON NAT'L. DETECTIVE AGENCY

BY. *A. F. Pinkerton.*

GENL. SUPT. WESTERN DIVISION.

F, T.

CHICAGO, APRIL 9TH. 1888.

H. B. STONE ESQ.,
    GENL. MNGR C. B. & Q. RY.
        CITY.

DEAR SIR:-

    FOLLOWING YOU WILL PLEASE FIND REPORT OF OPERATIVE'G. J. S'.

                    TUESDAY, APRIL 2ND. 88

TODAY IN ST. JOE.

    THINGS REMAINED QUIET YESTERDAY, DURING THE DAY AND EVENING. 20 MEN ARRIVED FROM CHICAGO, LAST NIGHT. THEY WERE MET AT DEPOT BY OPERATIVE, WHO ESCORTED THEM TO A HOTEL. AFTER THE MEN HAD SUPPER, ALL WERE TAKEN TO THE COURT HOUSE, WHERE THE SHERIFF DEPUTIZED THEM. THIS MORNING THE OPERATIVE TOOK CHARGE OF THE 20 MEN, AND PUT THEM TO WORK GUARDING THE SWITCH YARDS, AND SCAB SWITCHMEN, ALSO THE RY. PROPERTY. AT 8.35 A. M. CAPT. O'CONN -ER FROM BROOKFIELD TOOK A LOOK AROUND, AND SAID HE WOULD SEND O PR. -VEDER TO TAKE CHARGE FROM THE KAS. CITY OFFICE.

    THERE HAS BEEN NO TROUBLE THIS MORNING, AS THE MEN ARE KEEPING EVERY ONE OUT OF THE SWITCH YARDS.

        YOURS RESPECTFULLY.

    PINKERTON NAT'L. DET. AGENCY.
           BY.
           GENL. SUPT. WESTERN DIW

Chicago, April 21st.88

H.B.Stone Esq.,
    Gen'l.Mngr.C.B.& Q.Ry.
        City.

E.H.W.

Dear Sir.,

        Following you will please fuind report of operative "E.H.W."

                              Friday, April 6th.88

To day in St.Joseph,

        Ed.Hooton returned from Brookfield where he had been making arrangements for the Brakemen to strike. Williams a Brakemen on the K.C.has quit or struck, and he told the operative that all but three or four of the men had done just the same, and others he said are not Union men are now 'scabbing'. The operative asked him if the main line men had also gone out, he said he did not know, but Hopkinson told the operative they had, and if any attempt was made to reduce operators or clerks in general offices either in force or pay that they too would quit.

        After dinner the operative met Williams up town at the Gold Dust saloon and remained with him until 2 p.m. at which time he left the operative to attend the meeting. The operative was unable to learn from him what was to be the next move.

During the evening while the operative was at the Gold Dust saloon he met Sam Pillson and had two or three drinks with him but he knows no more about what is the next move than the operative does.

Saturday, April 7th, 88

This forenoon the operative was with Hooto. and Hurley and visited the different saloons. On their way to dinner Hooton and Hurley said they did not expect the Brakemen of the entire 'Q.'system would strike until after it was seen what the Knights of Labor did, but they said all arrangements were effected for them to do so in case Powderly did not call the Knights of Labor off, or in case the K of L. refused to obey Powderly's order.

Hooton is a member of the Brakemen's order and used to be a K of L. and says he thinks every man will respond if Powderly issues the order to quit, and that would take in freight handlers in Chicago and all along the line then if that dont have the desired effect the Brakemen will next be called out. Hooton also said that they had strong hopes that Mr. Stone would resign or be thrown out of office, and in that case then the contract with the Engineers would hold good no more. this, he said was told him by one of the 'scab' Engineers who said as long as Mr. Stone held his position he (the Engineer) would hold his and draw pay whether he made a trip or not unless discharged for cause. He said he thought two weeks at furtherest would tell the tale, but he did not look for the reinstatement of the old men as long as Mr. Stone retained his no ition for in case that the contract with the new man would be in ful force and could not be disregarded. After dinner the operative went to the "Spider" saloon and remained there until 4:30 p.m. to see if Hurley or Hooton came in.

After supper Hooton told the operative there was one thing he would have to do before he left St. Joseph and that was to whip the S--- of a B---- with the curly cap that took his place in the yards. The operative told him not to bite off more then he could chew, and remarked that he had made several grievous mistakes of that kind in his time, and always felt it his duty to warn others against making the same mistakes. Hopkinson said he would have a helper along, but Hooton said he though he was mad enough for him alone, and would not ask any one to assist him. Hopkinson and Hooton then jumped on a car and started off up town, and Pillson and the operative stopped in St. Charles Watkak Billiard hall and played several games of Pool with Lee Wilson, Tom Robertson, then went down to the Gold Dust saloon and remained there until 11 p.m. then went to their rooms and retired.

Sunday, April 8th. 88

To day being Sunday the operative was unable to obtain any information, as he has not got in with any of the striking railroad men who board at Mrs. Evans. The Brotherhood held a meeting this afternoon at which only members were allowed. Pillson told the operative that Hopkinson told him the boys were instructed just after Thomas & McDonald returned from Chicago to prepare themselves to stay out all Summer. Sam said they claimed there was money enough in the treasury and forthcoming to keep them out a year if need be, and wound up by saying some of them might prepare to stay out the balance of their life so far as getting work on the 'Q.' system went.

After dinner they went up to the Gold Dust saloon and also across from the Union Depot, but saw no one they knew. The operative did not go out of his room after supper, as it was raining and he thought he would only have but a poor chance to see any of the boys.

Monday, April 9th.88

This morning the operative went to the Post Office and received a letter from Mr.Merrill in which he suggested that operative should scatter seeds of dissention among the strikers, show the Switchmen that they were being made "Cats paws" of by the Engineers and Firemen and also that should the Brakemen and Freight handlers go out they also would figure in the same capacity.

The operative wrote C.M.Webber giving him a description of Ed.Hooton who has threatened to whip the "scab" who took his place as Asst.Yardmaster thinking he might be able if he knew Hooton to keep him from carrying out his threat.

At noon the operative had a short talk with Hooton and asked him if he had ever suspicioned that the Switchmen were being used as "Cat paws" by the Engineers. Hooton said he did not think such was the case it cant be, unless they go back on every promise they have made us, fo they have agreed to give us assistance in the future the same as they are giving them now.

The operative told him he thought it would pay the Switchmen to watch every move the Brotherhood made and at the first symptom of disregard for their promises to drop them. Hooton replied,"We are 21 years old, and will keep an eye on them."

P.Lavelle lodge No.92 of Brotherhood of railroad Brakemen give their third annual ball at Odd Fellows hall on Wednesday evening April 18th. and Hooton is selling tickets for same. He gave the operative an invitation (printed) and tried to sell him a ticket, he did not buy one, but thinks he shall as he believed it will be well worth the amount of money it will cost the company, as he must of necessity become acquainted with a number of Brakemen and no doubt a good many Engineers and Firemen will attend. Hooton and the operativ have made arrangements to attend the Opera House to see "Monte Christo" Thursday evening April 12th.

During the afternoon the operative met Hooton on Edmod St., and they went into Buffalo saloon together with anoth railroad man (did not learn his name) and played a few games of Pool, then left them as they had to go to see about the programs for the coming ball. He did not bring up the strike as he saw no good chance unless he started the subject himself.

Tuesday, April 10th.88

To day the operative was up to the Post Office twice but received no word from Mr.Merrill or Mr.Webber. He met Frank Stockwell at St.Charles Hotel in the bar room and played a few games of cards with him and Lee Wilson Proprietor of said saloon . Stockwell was on duty waiting upon a sick Fireman named Messer who used to fire engine 265 for K.C.Ry.Co.he is sick with the Measels and the Brotherhood boys take turn about sitting up with him. The operative had no opportunity of speaking to Stockwell in any confidential manner-but he is glad to have sort of formed his acquaintance for he is a Brotherhood man and may be of further service to him.

Wednesday, April 11th.88

To day the operative was about the St.Charles Hotel the greater part of the day. John Hopkinson being on duty caring for the sick Fireman who is stopping at the place. They played a few games of Pool with Robertson, and a young man named Ellison. Hopkinson has received his money and consequently is spending condiderable.

After supper Stockwell came into St.Charles Pool room and he, Lee Wilson, Harry Harris and the operative played 28 game of Pool which took them until 11 p.m. then Stockwell asked the operative to go with him to a dance saying a number of railroad boys were there and he had promised to meet them. They went to Adolph Gross's saloon on 2nd.near Felix St., where Stockwell paid one dollar which he owed. He then asked the operative to play him a few games of Pool, as he had not near played his game at the St.Charles. The operative did not care to play and told him so, but he insisted and so the operative beat him 12 games out of 18, and he felt satisfied. While playing Pool Stockwell told the operative that sometimes they (the Brotherhood) received encouraging news sometimes and other times none at all. He said for his part he had, had all

living. He did not know whether Powderly would order the men
(K.of L.)off of the 'Q.'system or not, but thought he would.
Stockwell said,'Striking is bad business and I only wish it
would end."

At the dance the operative was introduced to several railroad
men without knowing what roads they were from or in what capacity they worked. After entering the dance, railroad talk
was out of the question, and the operative did not attempt to
draw any one into it. The operative waited until 4 a.m. for
Stockwell to go home he promising all the while he would in
the next few minutes, then the operative left alone as Stockwell
went away with some woman.

  Before separating from Stockwell he promised to call
at his room tomorrow and said they would go around together in
the afternoon and attend the theatre in the evening.

           Thursday, April 12th.88

    To day the operative was too late for breakfast at
Mrs.Evan's so therefore went up town to a restaurant and had a
light breakfast there. Stockwell did not come around at 12
noon as he agreed to.

    The operative had dinner at Mrs.Evans' about 1 o'clock
and then went up 6th. St., to the barBer shop 2118 there he
heard a Brakeman named John Holland and a one legged man (who
u ed to carry water on K.C.Construction train but now is run-
a steam rock drill in K.C.quarry the operative should judge
from the way he spoke) talking about a certain Conductor (no
name mentioned) who used to run on trains 13 & 14 and was discharged for sympathizing with the Brotherh od Engineers in this

way this Conductor was asked by a passenger evidently at Omaha Transfer Depot how the strike was getting along and how the new Engineers were breaking in to which the Conductor replied "Oh they are doing fairly well I have got one of the 'Scabs' pulling me now.' This one legged man said the Engineer overheard this and reported it to the Master-Mechanic at Council Bluffs who being someway related to the Engineer made investigations and in doing so saw the passenger whom the Conductor had talked to and getting the Engineer's story corroborated by him therefore took steps to get the Conductor discharged . Hd land contradicted this and said he knew why the Conductor was discharged, but would not say why . The one legged man said he was in sympathy with the strikers but had to be areful what he said and to whom he said it or he would be discharged, but he wished Holland all sorts of success and said he hoped they would eventually freeze the Co.out . Holland said he was going to Kansas City Saturday and from there to St.Louis and was going to try and get work. Holland said he would try and "dead head" to Kansas City but if he had to, he could pay fare . The one legged man told of some Conductor on the K.C.who made him put up his fare and gave him a duplex receipt saying if he worked for the company and was coming into St.Joe on company's business they would refund him the money if he presented the duplex, that is the only one on the line makes me pay fare and I think his name was Moorehead or Moorehouse.

The operative received a letter from C.M.Webber askin to meet him at 9 this p.m. and the operative calculated to see him, but John Hopkinson and Sam Pillson called at his room and insisted on his going up town with them. They were joined by a Brakeman named Lewis (C.R.I.& P.man the operative thinks)and Chas.Merriman who walked up as far as the Union Depot with them. They had a couple of drinks at the Gold Dust saloon then Hopkinson excused himself and went over to the depot for a few moments saying he would return again. Sam wanted to go to see James O'Neil so the operative though by shaking Hopkinson he could easily get rid of Pillson. When it was time to go to the Opera House Sam and the operative went as far as St.Charles Hotel and then because he would not attend the show Sam would not and said he would sooner spend the dollar for Pool than to attend the show.

   They played Pool until 9:10 p.m. then the operative withdrew telling Sam he had a date with Queen at 9:15 p.m. Sam asked the operative if he would return if Queen did not show up, so the operative said he would.

   The operative arrived at the appointed place to meet Mr.Webber, but he had probably despaired of his coming, and so had left, as the operative did not see him. Sam and the operative went down to the Gold Dust saloon where they met Engineer Pierce with whom they had a drink, and about 10:30 p.m. the three of them started down 6th. St., towards their respective rooms. Sam started to talk by asking ,Well Mr.Pierce how about the strike?He said,"Oh nothing of any importance that is new,of course we are in daily receipt of encouraging news,and are determined to stay right where we are for a year,if we have to. The operative told him it was encouraging to know they were not bankrupt.

Bankrupt Pierce said, 'the A.T.& Santa Fe.boys are kicking because we dont call on them for money. He went on to say if he had, had his way no Boycott would ever have been started at all, but he would allowed the "Q." to receive and try to handle all the freight she could, then it would have been but a shot time before every engine on the line would have been smashed up. Of course we understood when we went out that the K.C. branch would make the best showing of any, for it is comparatively a straight road and easy to learn. He then spoke of the point where the freight train broke in two some weeks ago and the Conductor was killed why he said our Engineers here would dance H---- delight out of 50 loads there in Summer and 35 loads in winter, so it cant be much of a hill or sag either. Of course we know how many engines are smashed up, and there are plenty of accidents that the papers do not get a hold of at all . To show you he said, 'only a couple of days ago 5 dead engines were towed into Brookfield and about the same time 7 dead engines, a coach and a couple way cars all broke up were in one train over the B.& M.. We received in our first batch this morning 22 letters from different points along the line, and the facts about these dead engines were received in that way and given by eye witnesses s the company can's blind us by any false rumors they may start, as to what the railroad is doing'.

The operative met an Engineer and Fireman at dinner from the St.Joe & St.L.Ry.who said they knew quite a number of the boys (Brotherhood) were out looking for work. The Engineer said he had a Brotherhood in with him both ways on his last trip.

The Fireman said he had a passenger coming in to St. Joe who had been out looking for work without success.

Sam Pillson remained in front of operative's room for a few minutes after Pierce had left and said,'Now there is one of your brave Brotherhood engineers why he did not dare to come down 8th. St., alone any farther than the Gold Dust and would have remained up town all night if we or some one else he knew had not come along for company with him. Sam said he had heard Carter, Hopkinson, Williams, Hurley and Hooton speculating as to what and who the operative was. It was finally decided by Carter, Hopkinson, and Williams that he must be a detective. Sam said Hooton said it did not make any difference to him what he was, he did not propose to say anything to anyone he would not say to the whole world, and that if he could make more money working for Pinkerton than for the railroad company he would work for him. Sam also said he asked Carter, Williams and Hopkinson if the operative had ever tried to do any pumping or seemed desirous of making railroad and especially the strike the theme in his conversation and all agreed he had not but they were suspicious . The operative told Sam it made no difference to him what they thought but they owed him proper respect so long as he conducted himself in a way to expect it, and he would see they gave him his just dues. Sam spoke very highly of Hooton and said he was most fair among the lot of the strikers he knew.

Friday, April 13th. 88

To day the operate made two trips to the Post office but received no mail. He sent Mr. Webber a letter explaining how he happened to not keep the appointment of last night and told him he would meet him last tonight at 9 p.m. The operative spent the greater part of the day about the St. Charles Pool room (which joins St. Charles Hotel) and saw Fireman Carter there two or three times during the day as he was waiting on the Fireman who is ill. Carter ahted a little distant and although he drank with the operative he did not act as though he wished to have any conversation.

At 9 p.m. the operative met Mr. Webber and told him what Pillson said about the boys having suspicion of him and said he had a good mind to take them to task about it and act as though he had been grievously injured, by their giving vent to their suspicions. Mr. Webber said he thought it would be a good plan as it would either right him in their eyes or forever seal his fate, at least it would end the suspense at once. After leaving Mr. Webber the operative returned to St. Charles Pool room and in a few moments Stockwell came in and operatie gave him a drink. On their way to the Union Depot the operative talked to him about the throwing of stones through the coaches which happened a night or two ago, but he claimed to know nothing about it. He also brought up the death of Francis and said he believed the two Switchmen testified to lie about how near they were to Francis when the sad accident happened, but Stockwell said no, he had heard Hurley say before the Coroner s jury was called that one of the Switch men had told him just as he testified to. They stopped into the Gold Dust saloon on their way down and there met Sam Pillson and a railroad man named Richardson to whom he was introduced. Nothing transpired worthy of note.

In operative's report of yesterday he spoke of one John Holland (Brakeman) who was going to Kansas City and then to St. Louis looking for work. He confounded his name with others he heard during the day. He meant to say John Sommers instead of John Holland.

Saturday, April 14th.88

To day the operative went to the Post office twice, but received no word from either Mr. Merrill or Webber. He was at the St. Charles Hotel in Pool room most of the forenoon and saw Carter, but had but little to say to him. They played a few games of Pool with Thomas Robertson and Lee Wilson and then went down to the boarding house. On the way he met the Conductor who was laid off for refusing to act as Pilot when the Co. requested him to, and eventually quit. He spoke of the head end Collision that occurred last night in which engines 34 and 2 were smashed up a little and said he was glad of it and only hoped two passenger trains would come together He said the Kansas City Co. were fools for not giving in to the Brotherhood, and thought they must begin and feel that they are beaten.

At dinner time and at the table a painter named Hancock and a Brakeman named Williams got into a little spat about the number of wrecks happening now, and the number which happened before the strike. Hancock mantained that as many and as serious ones occurred before the strike as now. Williams was on the opposite side and got a little angry and said if the Brotherhood lost the fight that Hancock and all painters would be

Hancock finally sickened of hearing Williams talk and shut him up by saying that a man like him who up to three or four months ago was in the fence builders gang and were forced to go braking against his own will had but a small amount of experience and no business to talk about railroad wrecks or argue with a man of 15 years experience. At this time Hurley came in and took his seat at the table. The operative asked Williams if he belonged to the Brotherhood and he said no. The operative asked him if he honestly expected to ever be taken back in a body by the "Q." railroad company. He asked Who do you mean? The operative said, "Engineers, Firemen, Switchmen and Brakemen He said, "We expect if one man goes back every last one will. The operative said, "I thought it was generally given up as a settled fact that the "Q." could not do that without discharging these new men and thus lay themselves liable to suits for damage for not complying with the terms of the contract with the new men. I tell you Mr.Williams had I been a member of either the Brakemens or Switchmens Union and knew how the B.of L.E.& B.of L.F.looked upon a Brakeman or a Switchman they could not have pulled the wool over my eyes enough to have gotten him to quit work, and expecially after they had given out that this was their own fight and they did not want or need help from any outside organizations.unless they consolidated for all time to come and so did the boss in the Brakemens Union, and Powderly wanted to come in, but Arthur would not have him."

ing a few songs in the Barber shop they all except Dr.Boaz adjourned to the saloon next door where Sam and the operative remained until I a.m.   The operative could do no particular good by thus mingling except to form the acquaintance of and establish a friendly relation between himself and a different crowd of railroad men than those with whom he has been associating and thus by partially ignoring the first acquaintances he formed here, show them he has no special desire to associate with them or 'pump' them.

Sunday, April 15th.88

To day the operative met Pillson, Merriman, Stockwell Bob Trestein and Hopkinson this forenoon over on what used to be the Base ball part on So.4th. St., and played ball for a short time then adjourned to Andy Arnell's saloon and remained there until II a.m.   Their talk was Base ball and other topics of no interest to the C.B.& Q.Ry.Co.

At Dinner time Hopkinson asked the operative if he would put in with him and get a buggy and take a ride. The operative told him he did not want to go, so he tried to get Pillson to go. Sam said he did not have money enough or he would go Hopkinson said he would put in two dollars if the operative would put in one, and as he insisted on operative going he finally gave in and said he would do it, so went up town and got a rig and took a ride. He gave Hopkinson a good straight talking to about what he and the other boys had said about his being a detective, and told him he did not want the enmity of any of them and would sooner drop their acquaintances and not associate with them than to have them feel he was simply trying to

company by reporting same to them.   John said they had sort
of **suspicioned** him first, but after taking into consideration
how he had behaved, that he thought for the most part it was
dropped . He said, 'I would sooner tell you my secrets if I
had any than some of the Brotherhood boys.'   The operative
asked him again if he honestly thought the Brotherhood men
would get back, and he said he did and so would the **Brakemen**
and **Switchmen**, for he said not one will go back unless all do.
He denied that any one of the boys were now out looking for
work, all that had left were either away on business or else
visiting. Operative asked him if he meant on business for himself or the Brotherhood and he said both.   The operative
tried to show him how inconsistent it was to think the company
would discharge their new men for the old ones who had desert-
ed them , but John would or could not see it in that light.
The operative also spoke about attempting to use force and
said he had expected that, that would have been their tactics
before now. John said, 'No, we are cautioned against doing anything that will bring the Brotherhoods into disrepute.

   The operative is not able to learn of any more threat
being made, but dont feel that he is getting at the true in-
wardness of Hopkinson's or any of the boy's feelings .

   On the way to the Post Iffice this morning the operative overheard the St.car driver and another man talking a-
bout the whipping Engineer Hoffman got last night in St.car 26
and also the whipping Engineer Saeger got near Roachs' Grocery
store.   The operative understood from their talk that Saeger was not expected to live, but Hoffman was not so badly done

for . He also drew from their conversation that they were in sympathy with the men beaten as they denounced it as a brutal and cowardly affair$ In returning down So.6th. St.,the operative stopped in Chas.Clutters Barber shop and had a talk with him and Dr.Boaz about the "slugging"neither claimed to know anything about it except that it was said to be done by striking engineers ,while the operative's f. rst information led him to think the "slugging"had been done by Engineers now in the company's employ.

The operative spoke to Williams about it when he went to dinner, but all he knew he heard two shots fired after he had retired, and also heard the patrol wagon going fast ringing its gong.

About 2 p.m. the operative went to the Post ffice and on his return got into conversation with a young man on the St.car by the name of Geary who said he used to work in K.C.yards . He did not know much about the "slugging"of Saeger but said he understood he was badly beaten up and that he recognized his assailants and was going to have them arrested as soon as he was able to leave the house.

The operative called into the Gold Dust saloon and found Sam Pillson there. He has not been at work since the pay car was here, He began telling the operative about the "slugging Sager got last night down in front of Roachs' Grocery store . The operative told him he understood the "Scab"Engineers gave Saeger his beating;"scab"Engineers Sam said,didn't I see the old Engineers scattering in all directions after it was all right enough." About this time Curtis B. Wilson (the Fireman operative got acquainted with Saturday night) came in with Mr. Goodwin (Master-mechanic of C.K.& N.Ry.) and after he had introduced Sam and the operative to Mr. Goodwin and they all had treated, Mr. Goodwin left. The operative said to Wilson, "So you fellows got one of those S-of-B------and "slugged"him in proper shape did you.

A. You bet your life we did.

Q. Why do you say we did? you could not "slug" any one.

A. I can't look there .(and showed the operative his knuckle) which was somewhat swollen as though he had been doing some sort of pounding)

By this time it was near supper time, and as Sam Pillson wanted the operative to get five dollars for him from Mrs. Evans (as she keeps part of his money for him) the operative therefore left them abruptly and took a car for his room where he made

had said he struck Seager and claimed he hurt his knuckles on the stove in the Gold Dust saloon. Sam said to his face he had said he struck Seager and he need not deny it, you must be careful and not talk in such loud tones when so many are around. Wilson said he was alright and would take care of himself, and said, 'I was on the committee in Kansas City two or three weeks and you bet we did lots of dirt there that no one got onto.' He also said he helped to arrest the two Pinkerton Deputies who shot off their revolvers last night at the time Saeger was being beaten or about that time, and that they were now in jail. Pilson and the operative then left Wilson and started for the St. Charles Hotel. While in the street car while on their way Sam said, 'that (referring to C.B.Wilson) is one of the men I saw sneaking away from where Seager was "slugged" and he had a hand in it , and so did Charley Toppin I saw him sneaking away too. The remained at the St. Charles Hotel Pool room until 10 30 p.m. drinking and playing Pool and then they went down So. 6th. St., to Gold Dust saloon then got Sam to go and sleep with him.

Monday, April 16th. 99

During the forenoon the operative made a trip to t e Post Office and received a letter from Asst.Supt.'J.C.McG.' At the dinner table he met a C.K.& N. Engineer and F.reman and Williams a striking K.C.Brakeman. The operative began the conversation by bringing up President Perkins open letter to railroad employees who had stood by him and the company during this wrouble and said that does not look much as if you strikers were going to win.. William said such letters do not amount much that the company seemed to wholly ignore the fact that such organizations as B.of L.E.B.of L.F.B.of Ry.B.and the Switchmens Union were in existence and to an unbiased mind it said conslusively that forever more those organizations and the C.B.& Q.Ry.Co.wer: separate and in no way allied. Williams said,"From the way you talk one would suppose you were working for or in sympathy with the company. The operative said,'Now you better put it that I am working for the company for that is what you mean,only you are not man enough to come to my face and say so,but go around behind my back and give voice to mere suspicion and denounce me as a Pinkerton Detective,shame on you for your cowardice I have always thought you too much of a man to attempt to do another one harm behind his back,and I believe that is one of the cardinal teachings of your noble organization,but how poorly you follow its principles just because a man cannot agree with your views and arguments you denounce him as a detective and thus try not only to defeat him in making a livelyhood but put a stigma on his character that may take years to wear off".

    The K.C.& N.Engineer spoke of the number of wrecks of late and tried to show that on account of their occurrence the Engineers were incopenent. Operative said,'Now my friend let us look at it in this way,you take any road in the country and equip it from Engineer down to Brakeman with entire new men no one to act as pilot or no learning the road as is the rule at the same time attempt to run trains regularly and on time and what is the result. He admitted confusion and wrecks must

barrasment the fact that at every station men, women, and children pointing their finger at you crying 'scab' and perhaps an occasional stone thrown, and I tell you the oldest and best Engineer in the country would get rattled.' The Engineer admitted all the operative said to be true and Williams spoke up again and wanted to know how the operative explained their inability to get their injectors to work if they were competent Engineers. Operative said,'If I was as big a 'monkey' as you are and as hot-headed I would give you some crusty answer to your question, but I dont intend to so far forget myself, in the first place all ave not been bothered with their injectors, in fact only a few, and in my experience I have seen men grown grey haired with running an engine at a total loss to know what was the matter with their injectors and have to give up and have them taken apart and attended to by an expert. Operative said to the Engineer, you probably are a brotherhood man and an old runner (he said he had run an Engine 10 years) The operative asked him if what he stated was not rue and he said it was that he had been bothered in that way himself and thought every Engineer of experience would also say the same.

In the evening the operatative went to the 'Dime Museum' with Chas. Clutter (the barber across the way from his room) as he had heard him arranging with one of the B.of L.Firemen to meet him there. They remained at Museum during one performance and then left, not having seen anything of this Fireman. Clutter told the operative his name, but he does not remember it now. They went to the 'Spider' saloon and drank a couple of glasses of Beer then played Pool for a half or three quarters of an hour waiting to see if the Fireman would come then took street bar as far south as Union Depot and stopped into several saloons, but did not see the Fireman Clutter was to meet.

       Yours Respectfully,
      Pinkerton's Natl Detective Agency.
        by. *[signature]*
        Genl Supt.W.Div.
          A.C.

Chicago, April 24th. 88

H.B. Stone Esq.,
    Gen'l. Mngr. C.B. & Q. Ry.
       City.

C.M.W.

Dear Sir.,

    Following you will please find report of operative "C.M.W."

                           Saturday, April 7th. 88

To day in St. Joseph,

          At 6 a.m. the operative and his ment took breakfast and went on duty as usual. The night men reported everything quiet during the night. The operative halled on Mr. Merrill and had a talk with him in relation to the running of things here. He explained to him how the deputies conducted themselves and are robbing the company by neglecting their duty. Since the operative has been here he has been trying to get the men employed by the company as deputies working with a system but there appears to be no system in Harris their leader. The company has brought a Mr. Lawson one of their officers here to take Harris' place and the operative thinks things will be conducted different, as it was, it was a fraud. Mr. Merrill knew it was very bad, but had reasons for continueing them.

The men were all on duty during the day, and about 5 p.m. two switch engines left the yard to go to the Stock Yards to load cattle. They loaded about 40 car loads and were kept there until 11:30 p.m. when they started for home. Coming home they had a double headed train with No.12 yard engine ahead backing up . Two of our men rode on the foot beard of tender . When coming to the switch at the Grand Ave.crossing the switch was set for main line. The men saw it and called to Engineer to stop,but he did not get it in time and the tender run off the track.   J.E.Lennard a Deputy Sheriff and the watchman stationed here were both by the switch, and must have seen it was set wrong and left him go ahead and never attempted to throw it right. When she run off our men who was on the foot board asked the Deputy why they did not throw the switch right when they signaled to them and they saw it was wrong. Lennard said, "I am not here to throw switches if they dont know enough to attend to it let them run off it aint my business." They got the engine on the track and ready to pull out about 12 midnight and got up to the yard soon after.

At 2 a.m. everything was quiet, and the operative retied, leaving the night men on duty.

Sunday, April 8th.88

To day at 8:00 a.m. the operative had breakfast and had the men posted in the yards as usual. The night men reported everything was quiet during the night. The switchmen worked all the day as usual and all was quiet having no trouble at all.

At 4 p.m. the men went to supper and the operative formed around the hotel and yards up to 10:30 p.m. when he went to the hotel and retired for the night.

Monday, April 9th.88

To day as usual at 9 a.m. the operative had the men on duty in the yards. The night Sergeant Busey reported every things all quiet. At 10 a.m. a road engine No.30 running extra from Brookfield to St.Joe on H.& St.Joseph line Engineer Bundy, Fireman Belenger , and Deputy Sheriff Cline who meets the engines down the road and rides on them up into the yard was at or about the Rock Island crossing . There were three men standing at the crossing and some one threw an iron into the cab at the Engineer. The Deputy Sheriff stated that he knew the three men, but did not know which one threw it, but it must have been one of the three as there was no one else there. The operative reported this to Mr.Merrill and he ordered Cline to be at his office tomorrow at 8 a.m.

   Hughes' case was brought up before the Grand Jury this day, Cassidy , Morrison, and Bussy were up as witnesses , and the operative did not learn if they found the true bill or not as the attorney was not down town this evening.

            Tuesday, Ap'ri 10th.88

   To day the men were non duty as usual. Sergeant Bussy of the night squad reported everything quiet during the night. At 10 a.m. one of the yard shifting engines were over to Union Depot tracks with a car. Jack Burns the young man who attends the switch of Union Depot tracks called G.Tobin a Switchman of H.& St.Joe crew a S--o-f-A-B-----of a "scab" Tobin went for him and he ran for a link or pin to hit Tobin when Morrison and Metzzar two of our men interferred . Burns said he had a noti on to knock the brains out of the S--of-A-B----the police told him (Burns) if any of these men said anything to him he should split their head open they (the police) were with them and there would be nothing done to them. The operative saw Police officer No.5 and told him about the language Burns used in relation to the police and he got the sergeant of Police and they went down and saw Burns and was pretty sore over what he had said and asked him not to say anything about them as there had been a great deal said already and made trouble.

The operative was about the yards of the H.& St.Joe & K.C.yards and general office all the day. The men in Hannibal yard worked up to 9 p.m. and the men remained on duty up to the time those men quit, then the night men went on duty. The operative received a letter from operative 'E.H.W.' describing Ed.Hooton ex-yard master of K.C.yards as threatening to whip the man who took his position. Hooton is described as being about 30 years of age, 5 feet 5 inches in height, well build, weight about 135 pounds, red hair inclined to curl and small red mustache, florid complexion, dark clothes etc. Operative has seen this Hooton around the depot very often with a number of strikers.

Wednesday, April IIth.88

To day at 6 a.m. the operative arose and as previously requested by Mr.Merrill to have breakfast ordered for him at the Union Depot Hotel at 7:15 a.m. and to breakfast with him, the operative complied with his request. At 7:15 a.m. Mr. Merrill arrived and all was ready, and during breakfast they alked over the situation there. He has gone to Kansas City to be absent from here a number days and in case of necessity he wants to be communicated with as to affairs here. He left on 7:35 a.m. train.

All was quiet in the Hannibal yards during the night, but on K.C.road about one mile south of Francis St., station, engine 3I was bombarded with brick and a 38 Cal.bullet fired into the cab. The operative understands that detective Harris men were riding on the foot board of the engine in front and knew nothing of the damage done until after it was over. The trouble in the K.C.yards is they are about one and a half miles long and run on Fifth St., a public thoroughfare with houses on both sides of the street same occupied by a great number of men on strike who could stand in the door ways or yards of their own places and throw stones or shoot at train men.

Mr.Hohl Supt.K.C.yards requested the operative to have three Pinkerton men travel along the line of road this night until about I a.m. tomorrowmorning trying to get at the people who are doing the mischief, so he detailed three of the men for duty there tonight.

The men in the Hannibal yards worked u p to 8 p.m. everything was quiet during the day excepting that they had to drive several men off the company's property who presisted in remaining on the grounds, and there is no doubt wif our men were withdrawn they would not work one day in the Hannibal yards.

Thursday, April 12th.88

To day the operative had the men on duty as usual. Sergeant Bussy who was on duty during the night in Hannibal yards reported all was quietduring the night . Griffith with Friese and Brown reported they went out along the line of K.C. road and about 10 p.m. met Harris who has charge of the night men in K.C.yards . Harris told them that he had heard there was to be an attack on the trai. coming in at 11:30 p.m. at vicinity of Lakeville and requested that three men accompany him out there about four miles. They went with him walking along the road. They saw no one out there, so returned to the Round House of K.C.Co. arriving about I a.m.

Upon their arrival they learned from the men stationed there on duty as Deputy Sheriffs that there had been three bricks thrown through the window of the Round House about 12 midnight. The deputies ran out and searched in all directions but did not see any person about. Griffith reports that in going down the railroad from the Union Depot to K.C.Round House he met 39 Deputy Sheriffs on duty along the road, in returning at I a.m. he saw only four.

The operative was also informed that the passenger train was shotered with stoneson K.C.road above the Francis St. station the stones being thrown from the bluffs there being a deep cut at that point. The train men worked all day with good results in the Hannibal yards moving all card that arrived without trouble. There was one car damaged in K.C.yards this afternoon by switching engine running into the same, but nothing serious. Three men were detailed to patrol the K.C.road between Union Depot and Round House up to about I a.m.

The operative received a letter from Eppelsheimer Supt.K.C.to see Hill and Conn and have a talk with them. The operative wrote to both of them to meet him at certain points this evening, so he met Conn secretely and gave him all the information and points he knew. He then went to place appointed and met Hill he is not doing as well as Conn, but is doing the best he can. He next went to place set to meet operative 'E.H W.' at 9 p.m. and waited until 9:30 but did not see him so returned to yards, and all was quiet and at 12 midnight went to hotel and retired for the night.

Yours Respectfully,
Pinkerton's Natl Detective Agency.
by.
Genl Supt.W.Div.

A.C.

Chicago, April 25th, 88

H. B. Stone Esq.,
  Gen'l Mngr. C. B. & Q. Ry.
   City.

       C M W

Dear Sir,

  Following you will please find report of operative "C.M.W."

          Friday, April 13th, 88

To day in St. Joseph,

    The men were on duty as usual. The night Sergeant Bussy reported that all was quiet in Hannibal yards and heard one shot fired about 10:30 p.m. in K'C. yards. All the men were on duty during the day, and all was quiet, of course they have to put a number of trespassers off the company's property. At 8 p.m. the men quit work in the yards and the men all went to supper. At 7 p.m. the night men went on duty and the operative detailed three for duty in K.C. yards tonight with instructions for them to keep back off of railroad as much as possible and try to catch these parties throwing stones etc. The operative met operative "E.H.W." at the appointed place and explained to him how things were moving and the annoyance they caused the company, and gave him the names and descriptions of the parties and requested him to keep his eyes open for them etc. and after talking over the situation they separated, and the operative went to the yards, and after making a trip over the same he went to the hotel and wrote his report.

Saturday, April 15th. 88

To day the men went on duty as usual. Sergeant Bussy of the night squad reported all quiet during the night in the Hannibal yards. The operative had three men patrolling the K.C yard during the night and they reported that they were down along the K.C. road up to 2 a.m. There was quite a crowd of strikers hanging around 6th. St., about four blocks from the Round House Charles Smith being the center figure of the gang. Our men went down around and crawled up the back street in the vicinity of them and about 10:30 p.m. the strikers put out the street lights, but they attempted no depredations, and about 12 midnight adjourned. This meeting was on the public street there were thirty two Deputy Sheriffs in the yard during the night and twenty seven during the day.

This morning the operative met Huyler Sergeant of City Police and told him about this gang with Smith putting out the street lights, but he did not want to take any action in the matter, but admitted that it was a breach of the peace. The operative told him they put out the lights to cover them while throwing stones etc. Huyler said he thought the Deputy Sheriffs threw the stones.

About 9:10 a.m. as train No. 77 was pulling out of Hannibal yard when near the lower end of the yard this man Smith ran across the yard between the beats of Murphy and Morris and jumped on the caboose. Murphy ran after the train, but thought Smith was a train man.

In the afternoon the operative saw Smith and he admitted boarding the train, and said he knew the conductor (McGinnis) and wanted to go down to the crossing and did not know it was any harm.

The tough and central figures of the gang here around the depot are Tom Lynak, Charles Smith and John Dickey all Ex-Switchmen, they appear to do all the loud talking. This morning the company's officer who was in charge of the yard K.C. during the day reported that about 9 p.m. last night as a freight train was pulling out of K.C. yard a man jumped on one of the cars, he saw him jump on but thought he was a car man or Deputy Sheriff. In a few minutes the train was stopped by a cock or volve of air brake on one of the cars being opened. Lawson (the company's) officer) is almost sure it was Dickey who was on the train, for soon after this the latter and five others of his gang came up from that direction feeling very happy. They were whispering and niging each other and could not keep still. He wished to have Dickey shadowed in the evening, so operative sent operativ 'P.O³C.' to try and shadow Dickey and see if he could keep him to see what he does at night. The men in the Hannibal yards worked up to 8 p.m. The men had to drive several off the premises, otherwise all was quiet.

Sunday, April 15th.88

To day the men were on duty as usual. Bussy the night Sergeant reported that a great number of men congregated on 8th. & Mitchell Ave. near the central of Hannibal yards and were moving about up to 4 a.m. but did not go on company's property only to cross at Mitchell Ave. He stated as to Engineer Miller coming for him about 2 a.m. and he gave search for the two men, but they were gone. The three men on night duty in K.C. yard reported they had traveled about under cover as much as possible and all was quiet during the night.

The Deputy in Bunk room of Round House was discharged to day and operative put operative "D.P.O³C." on duty there tonight.

At I a.m. the operative was called up by a switchman stopping at the International Hotel saying that one of the Switchmen named George Sullivan had been up town drinking in the saloon at the corner of 8th.& Reddy Sts., and there was a crowd of strikers there and beat him and hit him with a brick and he was very bady hurt. The operativ had been at the hotel and cautioned all the Switchmen not to go away from the hotel, and he did not allow any of the 'P.P.' men to leave without permission. Sullivan has a pretty bad face, but nothing serious. The operative explained to Mr. Merrill all that had taken place and he said he w uld see the company's attorney about it and see if they can do anything with the parties.

                Yours Respectfully,

         Pinkerton's Natl Detective Agency.

                by.

                  Genl Supt.W.Div.

                    A. C

"I"

"Statement of James Sherleck Friday April 13th, 1888.
on C.B.& Q.strike.

"According to instructions received from C.M.Weber, Wendel and I proceeded to K.C.yards and looked about there patroling the place from Union Depot south of K.C.Round House. At 10:30 p.m. we were about 300 yards north of K.C.Round House when we heard a train that is engine and Caboose going south. I think it was either No.33 or 39 engines when about one hundred yards from us there was a stone thrown into the cab through the window. The Engineer fired a pistol shot in the direction from whence it came, and he saw a man on the track about ten feet away from the engine. The Engineer jumped down out of the engine cab and grabbed the man it was Deputy Sheriff who claimed he was there all the time, and did not see any one about. We ran up and learned the particulars then went to look to see if any one was around. We found a man whom I know to be Charley Smith a striking Switchman standing about one block away from the place the stone was thrown, he appeared as if he did not want us to see him, but I went up and held the lantern in his face and he is the same man I have seen around the depot and cross the yards. He usually wore a white derby hat, but this time he had on a black derby hat. I wanted Harris to arrest him, but he would not so I let him go. About 12 midnight as I was coming up 6th. St., I saw this same man come out of a saloon on 6th.St., and go into the Gold Dust saloon and then he had on his white hat. I felt sure that this was the man that threw the rock jor if he did not throw it he knows who did I saw the man to day and he shunned men

The stones might have been thrown from some house, as there are houses all along both sides of the street there. Otherwise nothing happened. There are a number of these fellows running around all night.

C.M.Weber and I looked up this man with the white hat on and found he goes by the name of Charley Smith, is married and came from Nebraska. Summers says that his right name is Clancy and that his father and he murdered his mother up in Nebraska, and when he left there changed his name. He formerly worked for St.Joseph and Grand Island road as section man in the floating gang. Thinks he lives in Beatrice Nebraska. He is a hard case.'

A.C.

Statement of Thomas Govin for Sunday, April 15th. 1888 on the C.B.& Q. strike.

"At 10 a.m. while riding in a street car going up town to church, I sat next to an old man who was short and stout dark complexion, and dark beard. He said his name was Demsey and used to fire on the Hannibal road. In the course of conversation he said the men had been keeping quiet, thinking they would be able to win, but now they see there is no show and and they were going to use force. He said the yard is full of men at work who would not be there only for the Pinkerton men, and he heard they were going to send half of them away and as soon as they did this, the boys were going to mob the rest, and they thought they could get away with 10 of them.

This man done condiderable talking about the company and he stated all the men acknowledged they were beat, and by having the Pinkertor men here to protect the 'scabs' is what done it. He did not know Govin as he saw he was Irish and had no idea he was one of them.

Statement of Wm. Miller for Sunday, April 15th. 1888 on the C.B.& Q. strike.

"I an Engineer in H.& St.Joe yards and run night shift ter. Last night I was in the bunk room of the Round House with several others in bunks. At 2 a.m. two men came into the Round House one carried a lamp the other a long knife. The man with the lamp was Anderson, a young man that used to whip engines here. The other was a tall slim young man with light clothes. Anderson came to my bed and flashed the lamp in my face which awoke me. He then said, 'I want you to take en gine out." I thought perhaps they did want the engine out, so I reached under the bed for my shoes and I suppose they thought I reached for a gun and they both ran away. Cuthbertson a Deputy Sheriff should have been in there on duty this is his post, but he was not here. I ran out to get the three 'P.P.' men, and when we returned the two men had gone and Cuthbertson came around a short time afterwards and said he heard a noise outside on the other side of the Round House and had gone around there, and while there the men came in. In the afternoon I saw Anderson and he said he was drunk and did not know what he was doing and did not know the man that was with him with the knife."

Pinkerton's National Detective Agency

FOUNDED BY ALLAN PINKERTON
WM. A. PINKERTON, Gen'l Supt. Western Division. CHICAGO.
ROBT. A. PINKERTON, Gen'l Supt. Eastern Div. NEW YORK.
1850

"WE NEVER SLEEP."

OFFICES
CHICAGO, 191 & 193 FIFTH AVE., WM. A. PINKERTON, Supt.
DENVER, McPhee & Wilson Block, CHAS. O. EAMES, Supt.
PHILADELPHIA, 44 SOUTH THIRD ST., R. J. LINDEN, Supt.
NEW YORK, 66 EXCHANGE PLACE, GEO. D. BANGS, Supt.
BOSTON, 42 & 44 COURT ST., JOHN CORNISH, Supt.

ATTORNEYS FOR THE AGENCY:
CLARENCE A. SEWARD, NEW YORK.
LEWIS C. CASSIDY, PHILADELPHIA.
D. W. MUNN, CHICAGO.

CONNECTED BY TELEPHONE.
ST. PAUL, UNION BLOCK, W. J. LOADER, Supt.
KANSAS CITY, 105 & 107 WEST SIXTH ST., C. H. EPPELSHEIMER, Supt.

Chicago, April 26th. 88

H. B. Stone Esq.,
    Gen'l. Mngr. C.B. & Q.R.R.
        City.

C M W

Statements of Roach & Hoffman

Dear Sir.,
      Following you will please find report of operative
"C.M.W."

                                Monday, April 16th. 88

To day in St. Joseph,

              The men were on duty as usual. Bussy the night Sergeant reported that the night was unusually quiet Wilkinson, Doherty, and Murphy who were on duty in K.C. yards reported everything quiet over there.

      This morning the operative took Engineer Wm. Miller the man who was attacked in the bunk room on Saturday night) to Judge Strong the company's council, and stated the case to them and they said they would look the matter up and see if there was a show of convicting Anderson and his partner. Strong also stated that the Grand Jury had found a true bill against Hughes for attempting to throw the switch and he would be brought to trial soon.

      To day at 12:30 p.m. as Engine No. 62 extra from Brookfield arrived in Hannibal yards a piece of iron was thrown into the cab of locomotive and broke the window. Fireman James Ma__ __on saw the man throw the iron, but could not reco erganize him again nor give any description of him. J.W. Shortit the Engineer did not see the man. The iron was thrown from the west side of the Hannibal track about a quarter of a mile below the Hannibal yards. The operative sent Sherlock and O'Connor down there to set about under cover as much as possible and try and get these parties. While there engine No.1.of the St.Joseph Terminal Company came down with freight train. Their tracks run along close to and west of Hannibal tracks parallel with same. As this was moving south, at the same point engine 62 was assaulted at the tressell a half of a pin was thrown from the top of this train at these men, and struck the car close by them and made a large dent in it. There was five men on top of the car of this train, some sitting on the brake, and when our men looked at them they were all busy at work, and it is impossible to say which one of them threw the pin but one of them did it, as there was no other person in sight and it could not have come from any other point. All these men and the Rock Island people are very bitter.against the Hannibal people.

To day a number of the railroad men got their pay, and there were several of them drunk towards evening and as they are beginning to feel their lost cause for all here plainly see they are badly beaten, so the operative had three men on patrol duty in the yard and one man on duty in Bunk room of Round House where train men sleep, and tonight has five men to sleep in the Round house to be ready to jump out at a moment's notice if needed which will save time of going to the hotel.

Tuesday, April 17th. 88

To day the men were on duty as usual and the operative sent two men down the railroad to the lower end of town to the vicinity tof where the engines had been molested by stone throwing etc.

Bussy reported everything quiet in the Hannibal yards during the night. The operative telegraphed Gen'l.Supt.of the iron throwing into engine to day, then went to the general offie on business and there learned that Engineer Sager who was beat last night down town was seriously hurt. The operative then went to 2600 So.6th.St.,where Saeger was way layed and from general inquiries in vicinity without going into any investigation learned that last night (Monday) about 7:40 p.m. and Engineer named Hoffman boarded a street car about the vicinity of K.C.Round House and was going home. In the vicinity of 6th.& Hickeyy Sts.,three strikers boarded the car. There being no other passengers in the car one of them sat down beside Hoffman and suddenly struck him in the side of the head with a piece of iron or brass knuckels and knocked him down and jumped on him,but he got away with little damage. Soon after this happened as Engineer Saeger was at the corner of 6th. St.,four men took him unaware and one hit him in the head with a brick and when he fell the lot of them jumped on him and beat him very bad.

From what the operative heard in general talk it seems that ex-employees C.H.Tophan,Nelson,Caruthens ,Carson Fireman and Fred Murray done the beating of these men,Priestly and Roderick were two of the men who were on the street car and there were a number of the other strikers in the gang.

About II a.m. while Sherlock was going down the railroad opposite the Terminal Round House at the point where the engines have been attacked a large iron nut was thrown from the Terminal building or the coal shute which is about 30 feet high. it I fell within a few feet of him, but he could not see any person about there. The two men were down there all the day and nothing else occurred.

The operative met Charles Smith an Ex-switchman who jumped a train and rode out the yards previously stated and the operative gave him a lecture. Smith stated that in the cours of conversation that Wednesday night the Brakemen's brotherhood gives a ball and they expect to have a big time and after the ball he is going to leave town and go to St.Paul to look for a position and expects to get work there, and quite a number will leave next week.

At 2 p.m. the operative went to the general office and met Messes Merrill and Hohl and explained to them what he had heard. The yard men worked up to 7 p.m. and nothing occurred worthy of note.

In the evening the operative received a letter from Strong & Mosman Attorney's for the railroad company stating that Deputy Sheriff Craig told them that he had called to see the operative about the witnesses in Hughes case to subpoena them. The operatow stated by letter that the whole of this man's statement was all a lie no one ever spoke to him on the subject and he would call and see them tomorrow.

Wednesday, April 18th. 88

   To day the men were on duty as usual. The night Sergeant Bussy reported all quiet during the night.

   The operative went down to the lwer end of the town and took statement from Roach the store keeper in the Saeger assault and called and talked with a number of people in the vicinity and was informed by different ones that Mitchell who resides first house south of Self's store saw all the men when running away.

   Mary Cordin who resides back of South 6th. St., near lower end said she saw the men and knew two of them and could swear to them.

   Robert Iberton who works at Street car stables saw the men running up the street and no doubt knew them. Mrs. Hammond resides corner of Cedar & Bartlett Sts., was on So.6th. St., and the men all passed her.

   Those people with a number of others the operative had intended to visit and interview . By this time it was 12:30 p.m. and the operative went to dinner, after which he called at Mr. Hohl' office and met Hoffman whom the operative took a statement from and met the company's attorneys and had a talk with them. They want to be very sure of a conviction before they do anything. They propose to have Hoffman with the street car driver see this man and if the three men agree that he is the right man then arrest him otherwise let him go. They stated that Hughes had to day pleaded guilty and was sentenced for two years to the penitentiary . When the operative got through here it was 4 p.m. and too late in the day to

go up town to investigate besides he had other work to attend
to. When the operative arrived at the hotel for supper he
received a letter from operative Hill and Supt.Eppelshiemer
the latter stating he had left Kansas City on the 4 p.m. train
and former requesting the operative to meet him at 8 p.m. on
the corner of 8th. & Francis Sts., as he had something of importance to report to him.

At 7:5 p.m. Eppelshiemer arrived and they had supper, after which they proceeded to meet operative Hill . They waited around until 9 p.m. but as he did not show up they retrned to the Hannibal yards . The operative was around until II p.m. when he went to the hotel and wrote his reports.

Thursday, April 19th.88

To day the men were on duty as usual , and Sergeant Bussy reported that there was a a stone thrown against the Round House from the vicinity of Union Depot, otherwise all was quiet during the night.

The operative called at the general officer and Mr. Hohl decided not to have an open investigation of the Seager and Hoffman assaults, but they propose to ask the Grand Jury to be called together and make a statement to them of all the low business that is going on in town and have them to subpoena witness and hear them and through that channel have the Grand Jury to convict the parties who assaulted these men so the operative discontinued the investigation.

All is very quiet here up to the time of writing at I II:30 p.m.

Friday, April 20th.88

  To day the men were on duty as usual and the night Sergeant reported all quiet during the night. Have got rid of all the Deputy Sheriffs in Hannibal yard now excepting two on day duty and three on night, and there has been a large cut down of same in K.C.yards.

  The Grand Jury of County court was called to day, and Strong & Mossman are going to present their case to them for consideration, and try and find bills of indictments against some of these lawless fellows.

  This evening at 8 p.m. the operative met C.F.Curtis operative of Kansas City who came to take Hill's place in secret work and the operative gave him all the points and advice in his power to enable him to make a success.

  The men worked in Hannibal yard on switch engine to night up to II:50 p.m. and consequently the operative had all the patrol out on duty.

        Yours Respectfully,
        Pinkerton's Natl Detebtive Agency,
          by J
           Genl Supt.W.Div.
            A.C.

'Statement of Michael Roach for Wednesday, April 18th, 1888 on the C.B.& Q.strike.'

'I reside and keep a Grocery store on the N.E.corner of So.6th.& Cedar Sts., St.Joseph. I have redided here for one year. On Monday night April 16th.1888 at about sundown they had just lighted the lamps it was between 7 & 8, I was in the store. Seager Engineer of K.C.road was in my store and paid my a bill he owed me, after which he went out. I heard him shout "My God" or something like that about a minute after he left. I was busy behind the counter, but I ran to the end of building. The deor was open and I saw three or four men have a hold of Saeger dragging him from the corner of Cedar St., up 6th. St., and I saw them strike or throw him down and struck him as he fell and kicked him after he was downthen o e large man who was about 6 feet tall, stout build, I cannot say as to his complexion, he wore a dark suit. He lifted Saeger up and looked at him as though to see if he was dead, and seeing he was not, dropped him down and kicked him in the neck or chest when Saeger's head fell back as if he was dead. There was quite a crowd of persons present and saw them :beat the man. There must have been 18 or 20 men around before the man that was beating him ran away. I heard that Cunningham a sxkkxx Policeman had shot at them while running. I locked the doors and kept every one out for some time. After they were gone I opened the doors and they brought Seager in my store. Deeputy Thomas and others brought him in. Saeger did not say anything for some time, and when he did speac he said two men grabbed him from the rear and another struck him with a rock. I did not hear him saw whether he knew any of them or not. I do not know any of the men that wery in the crowd beating him and identify any of them excepting the man who kicked him the last. There was two smaller men who first threw him over to examine him to see if he was dead or not. They were dressed in dark clothing could not tell anything about it as it was very quickly done and the gang was off.

There was present in my house and about the corner at the time of the attack Ed.Drake,& Wife, reside 1309 So.4th. St., Widow Hill's son live on Hickery & 4th. Sts., William Thomas Deputy he came there at the time they ran away. My Son Bela Roach was in the store at the time and there was also quite a number of others, and they all had to wait a little. There was a man named James Kennedy an ex-fireman who was in the store at the time and saw Saeger there. He appeared to be very restless and went to the door alnd looked out a number of times and just left about one minute ahead of Saeger. Kennedy must know who done the beating and who was there I dont see how he can help but know as they left almost together. James Kennedy lives on 4th. St., near Walnut St., he is in with the B.H. people and one of their leaders, and stands high among them. Mary Cordin who lives south west from Ringleton House told me she saw the men running and knew some of them, one or two of them and could swear to them. She works in the woolen mill. My hired girl Annie Annfield stated she saw two men run up Cedar St., shouting 'scab' and they must have got there before the men ran away. She would know them again if hhe saw them. they came from down Cedar St.,

"Statement of A.M.Hoffman Wednesday, April 18th.1888.
on the C.B.& Q.strike.

"I reside at Leavenworth Kansas and am Engineer on No.15 K.C.train on Creston branch, have been in the employ of the company since the 28th. of February 1888. On April 16th.1888 I left the K.C.Round House about 7;30 p.m. to preceed to the Beacon House on 3rd.St., where I board. I proceeded to 6th. St. and bearded a car No.26 of that line for home. Upon entering the car there was no passengers aboard, no Conductor in the car and only the driver with the front door closed. After riding about half a block three men boarded the car. I occupied the forward west corner of car and one man about 30 years of age, 5 feet 11 inches in height, heave, stout build, light complexion, light mustache, wore full grey or pepper or salt suit of clothes, black slouch hat, I did not notice anything else of th man. He entered the car stood up about half a minute then sat down on same seat with me. At the same time another man and companion of the first entered the car and sat opposite to the first man. He was about 40 years of age, 5 feet 7 inches in height, stout build, black mustache, red faced, dark complexion, he wore a dark suit, black derby hat, he wore a gold vest chain and either a charm on it or a pin on his vest close by the chain . There was a third man entered the car, but stood in the doorway he was about 26 years of age, tall and slim, fair complexion, dark mustache, wore dark clothes, dark slouch hat, I did not notice any jewelry. When the car pulled out the man on rear platform said, 'Let us get off boys and go up and next car, the one who sat by my side said no, let us go up on this car. There was nothing more said.

The car had gone about one block when opposite the car stables the man who sat by me said to me,"are you working for K.C.? I said yes, then he struck me in the right side of my head which stunned me and knocked me down. I did not realize anything for a few minutes, then he struck me on the nose and it commenced to bleed. The threw him off and got up pulled the door open or the driver opened the door. I got out the front end of the car on the west side and as I was going through the door this man struck at me again, but did not hit me. The three men left the car on the east side by rear door. I saw the three men going south on 6th. St., in the middle of the road. I do not know if either of the other two struck me or not, but I think the man who sat opposite to me kicked me while the No.1.man was on top of me. I then got on the car again and went home and on the way had a talk with the driver(William Adams)who said the first that he knew he heard a racket on the car and tried to get the door open, but could not for it stuck or they were against it. When he got the door opene I was about on my feet and got out. The three men when they got off the car had some talk and No.1.man wanted to go after me again, but the others stopped him and hurried him back that is all he said about it.

Yesterday morning Tuesday April 17th.while I was going down to work riding on the street car I saw No.2.man the one that sat opposite to me in the car sitting in front of a saloon on the west side of 6th. St., at about the point where these men left the car after assaulting me, and I saw this same man at this saloon a number of times before this. Going down on in the car by me, and this No.2 man spoke to a man who was standing in the door and both looked over at me . I can identify the three of them or positively the two that were in the car I saw No.1 man several times before this too, he was one of a number who tried to buy me off from work at this time he was in company with Dick Pierce an Engineer.

Chicago, April 27th.88

H.B.Stone Esq.,
    Gen'l.Mngr.C.B.& Q.R.R.
        City.

D.P.C'C,

Dear Sir.,

Following you will please find report of operative 'D.P.O'C.' on shadowing Dickey.

Saturday, April 14th.88

To day in St.Joseph,

About 3:20 p.m. Asst.Supt.'C.M.W.' relieved the operative and instructed him to go to the vicinity of the Union Depot and see if he could find Dickey and shadow him. The operative then went around the neighborhood and visited the saloons opposite the depot, but did not see Dickey. About 6:50 p.m. the operative saw him standing on the corner of 6th. St., talking to two men and he had his little boy with him. After he left the men he crossed the street and passed through the depot, noded his head to several men standing at the station and walked towards the yard of the H.& St.J.R.R.meeting one of the employees of the yard whom the operative understands to be the foreman of the construction gang and remained talking to him for over five minutes. The man was about 37 years of age, 5 feet 8 inches in height, meddum build, weight about 160 pounds, dark complexion, brown hair, were dark pants, blue sack coat, blue vest, black slouch hat. Dickey then passed through the yard accompanied by his boy and met another man who walked up Mitchell Ave. with him. The man left Dickey at the street this side of the railroad, and Dickey turned the corner of the next street and the operative could not see which house he entered, nor can he tell what street it is, as he did not see any names up. Dickey arrived home about 7:10 p.m. and the operative did not want him to see him in the neighborhood as he may know him to be one of the guards, and as there was no place to take cover on account of the railroad running through this st he returned to the hotel and had supper, after which he walked up Mitchell Ave. intending to loiter around the neighborhood of Dickey's house, but as he saw that he would attract attention and that he could not get good cover he returned to the depot and remained around the station. He saw the gang Dickey generally associates with at the station, but Dickey was not there. One of this gang appears to be a kind of a "picket" he is a man about 40 years of age, 6 feet in height, slim build, dark complexion, black hair, bushy beard, dark eyes, dresses in blue flannel suit, sack coat and black derby hat. He takes an active part in the strike as he boards all the trains arriving, and looks into each car and peers into every man's face who gets off the train and walks up to the engine and looks into the cab. He is always around the station going from one group of men to another talking to them and acts as if he has some authority more than the rest of them.

The operative visited the saloons opposite the depot several times during the day, but did not see Dickey.

-3-

The operative then went down 6th. St., some 15 blocks and remained around the neighborhood visiting every place where he thought he would find Dickey, but did not see him, and not finding him up to 11:15 p.m. he discontinued and retired.

Dickey is about 36 years of age, 5 feet 7 & 1-2-inches in height, medium build, weight about 150 pounds, dark complexion, light brown hair, light brown mustache, wore dark pants, a faded brown cardigan jacket with large buttons, brown derby hat and always carries a stick.

        Yours Respectfully,
      Pinkerton's Natl Detective Agency.
        by. *W. C. Pinkerton*
         Genl Supt. W. Div.
         A.C.

Chicago, April 28th.88

H.B.Stone Esq.,
    Gen'l.Mngr.C.B.& Q.R.R.
        City.

E H W

Dear Sir.,

    Following you will please find report of operative 'E.H.W.'

                            Wednesday, April 18th.88

To day in St.Joseph,

    The operative was at the Post Office twice during the day, and when returning to his room the second time about 4:30 p.m. he stopped in the Gold Dust saloon on So.6th. St., opposite Union Depot and saw C.B.Wilson. Wilson was sober and the only conversation they had was about the Brakemen dance tonight. The operative did not mention yesterday's talk to him at all as he thought it best to wait and see if he would bring up the subject himself. The operative treated him and left him with the understanding that he would be at the ball .

The operative saw Hopkinson and Williams at meals to day, but merely passed the time of day with them. At the ball he met Ed.Hooton, Hurley, Stockwell, Wilson, Chas.Clutter and three or four other Brakemen, that Hooton introduced him to whose names he does not remember . The operative invited Hooton, Hurley, and Stockwell out to take a drink, and after drinking, Stockwell proposed a few games of Pool. During the progress of the game the operative got Hooton to one side and told him he had heard of the talk he (Hurley)Williams, Carter and Hopkinson had about him and he said it made him feel sore to think he should stand it such a light when he so justly deserved to be better thought of than that. Hooton said,'I told them not to say any more about it, but to wait and see if you done or said anything to justify them in suspicioning you. Have they said anything more? The operative said,'I dont know and that's what I dont like if I knew they would only say what they had to say to my face I would not bare, but a man cannot guard against one who strikes behind his back you know." He said,'No, and that is not my principal, as far as I am concerned, it would make no difference to me if you were seven times a Pinkerton man as long as you show me proper respect, and you can demand the same from me, and I told those fellows that they did not have to tell you any-thing even if you should ask them and also said it was not right to denounce a man until they were doubly certain.'

There being such a crowd at the hall the operative did not remain only until 11:30 p.m. and then went home.

Thursday, April 16th.08

The operative made two trips to the Post Office during the day and one in the evening. In the afternoon C.B. Wilson and a friend of his was at the St. Charles Pool room when the operative was there. They got into a game of Pool together and played until about 5:30 p.m. when Wilson and the operative started alone down So. 6th. St., On the way to the rooms Wilson told the operative that the Engineers had been raised from $60.00 to $80.00 per month and the Fireman from $40 to $60.00 per month. He also said he paid the boys here; that $5000.00 was sent here and $5000.00 out in Nebraska for B.& M. men, and that he was Recording Secretary and Receiver for their (B.of L.F.)lodge and also Magazine Agent and he showed the operative an Express receipt for $163.00 sent to Eugene V. Debbs collections from Magazine subscriptions. He then asked the operative what his occupation was and the operative told him he expected to go firing if this trouble ever ended, but that he was getting sick of waiting so long, for he was afraid he might get "froze out" and that he had been handling Stationery and hoisting engines for the past three or four years and before that, he had fired on the C.St.Paul M.& Omaha Ry. with headquarters at Eu. Claire Wis. and his character would bear investigation and he invited any one to correspond with Martin Cuddy at Altona Wis. where the C.&St.P.M.& Q.Ry.Co. have their headquarters to learn if he was not stateing the truth(Martin Cuddy is Chief of B.of L.F. at Altona and he took it for granted Wilson would know this or could find he was right by referring to the B.of L.F's.Magazine)and still some of your D-----S--of- B------of Brotherhood Firemen, Brakemen, and Switchmen have reported it around that I am a detective. ' The operative continued by saying, 'You will doubtless say I am using pretty strong language , well I admit it is strong, but it does not half express my contempt for one who upon his own suspicion and merely conjectures will start a report about a man with nothing of the slightest nature to build upon that may take years to give the lie to by living it down and had it not been for the insig-

it in a manner that would not have been at all pleasing to them Wilson said, 'I heard it intimated that you are a detective, but I never gave it much thought, but I do not uphold any one in starting such a report unless they have good grounds for doing so.' The operative said, 'The only grounds they have is because I dont happen to think as they do about your chances of getting back on the 'Q'system to work, and in talking with them have two or three times expressed my views, for a man with an opinion who dare not express it is not entitled to one. My sympathy has been with the boys from the first, but I would not allow my sympathy to get the best of my judgement and prejudice me, no sir, Wilson yours is a lost fight and there is no need of trying to conceal it.' Wilson said, 'Oh, no, we dont give up the ship yet.' The operative asked him how he could say that and be honest to himself. He said, 'Well we know the company is loosing money every day and their motive power and rolling stock is getting terribly run down and we dont believe the Stockholders will submit to this much longer, it would not surprise me if the 'Q'did not fall into the hands of a Receiver I tell you when you cut off the regular dividends and in their stead levy monthly assessments you soon will hear a howl from Stockholders , so far we have refrained from any acts of violence. The operative said, 'Except in the case Pat Brown Saeger, Hoffman .' He said, 'of course the Brotherhood will get blamed for those things whether they do them or not.' The operative said, 'It is a pretty conclusive evidence when two or three men admit they are Brotherhood men and go before a Police Justice and p ead guilty and pay a fine and besides that you know it was Brotherhood men who 'slugged' Saeger.'

He said,'I dont know any such thing.' The operative said,'You do, for you as much as told me the other day in the Gold Dust saloon that you yourself helped to slug Seager.' He said,'I was drunk then.' The operative said,'Yes just drunk enough to make you think it smart to boast of it, and now for some reason you try to go back of what you said.' He said,'I may have said so, but I did not have anything to do with it, and dont know anything about it.' The operative called him a liar and told him he would think much more of him to come out like a man and say he knew all about it, but did not want to talk about it and still he insisted he was ignorant of who did it.

Wilson and the operative met after supper at the St. Charles Hotel and then went over to the Monarch Billiard and Pool room and played a few games of Pool then went down to the Gold Dust saloon and had an Oyster stew, after which they went home.

       Yours Respectfully,
      Pinkerton's Natl Detective Agency.
        by.
         Genl Supt.W.Div.
           A.C.

Chicago, May 31st., 1892

M... ...th...,...

Gen'l. ....

City

Dear Sir:--

...... I... you ... please ... ...port of Operative 'J.O.'

Tuesday, May 24th., 1892

To-day at St. Joseph, Mo.

At 6.30 ...... the operative relieved the day watch visited the guards at their different posts and found them attending to their duties. Nothing unusual occurred while the operative remained on duty.

Wednesday, May 25th., 1892

As reported yesterday, everything is quiet here an.. .... of any kind.

Yours respectfully,

Pinkerton Nat'l. Detective Agency

by ....

Gen'l. Supt. W. Div.

Chicago, June 4th., 1898

H. B. Stone, Esq.

    Gen'l. Mngr. C.B. & Q.R.R.

        City

Dear Sir:--

    Following you will please find report of Operative
"C. M. T."

                         Saturday, May 28th., 1898

To-day in St. Joseph

    At 8 A. M. the operative relieved the night watch who reported everything quiet, during the night, was around the yards for some time, then proceeded to the General office and saw Mr. Merrill, and Supt. Hohl, turned over to Mr. Hohl the commissions and badges belonging to the Company. Mr. Merrill told the operative he was perfectly satisfactory.

    At 6.25 P. M. the operative boarded the train for Kansas City and arrived at Kansas City at 9.15 P. M.

                Yours respectfully,

                Pinkerton Nat'l. Detective Agency

                by

                    Gen'l. Supt. W. Div.

www.ingramcontent.com/pod-product-compliance
Lightning Source LLC
Chambersburg PA
CBHW031605110426
42742CB00037B/1232